Ue

EXIT

The last year with my father

ISBN 978-1-9163644-3-1

The book was first published in German under the title
Ausgang: *Das letzte Jahr mit meinem Vater*

This edition is a translation by Iris Hunter, Cambridge

Cover design by Duncan Bamford,
Insight Illustration Ltd
http://www.insightillustration.co.uk/

Copyediting by Jan Andersen
http://www.creativecopywriter.org

Republished in English by:

PERFECT PUBLISHERS LTD
23 Maitland Avenue
Cambridge CB4 1TA
England
http://www.perfectpublishers.co.uk

'No One Here Gets Out Alive'

Jim Morrison

About the Author

Writing – time and again

'We cannot help it', my cousin Bernhard Schlink once told an audience at a reading, referring to the descendants of our grandfather. He is right: writing has been in our blood for generations and it is a passion that drives us. Grandfather, known for being stubborn, posted many 'letters to the editor', produced pamphlets and wrote the family history. Grandmother kept a diary up into her old age. My father published non-fiction books on business management. My brother and my cousins all write books. Obviously, we cannot help it. Fate steered me, via some detours, into journalism. When I received a letter from a reader, who told me that my article had brought tears to her eyes, I felt that I had made it, even though it took another few years before my passion found its way into published books. And here I am, writing and writing . . .

Ueli Oswald, born in Zurich in 1952, trained as a photographer in London and Hamburg, before studying ethnology and journalism at the University of Zurich. After ten years as a journalist, he became Editor-in-chief of the renowned literary monthly *NZZ Folio*. He launched his book-writing career with *Ausgang*, first published by Edition Epoca. The success of this book put Ueli Oswald at the centre of the issues associated with assisted dying. After a series of perceptive memoirs and biographies, he published his first novel in 2018, *Das Vergessen ist ein Dieb!*

Preface

Why this translation?

It is not only my small, Swiss world, which is silent about dying, death and, particularly, voluntary death. Unfortunately, death remains a taboo in many countries and societies. We can only regret this because it shuts out one of the most significant and important aspects of our life.

I decided to publish a translation of *Ausgang* when dozens of readers sent me letters thanking me for my openness. There was only one negative reaction among all the messages: one reader felt that such matters do not belong in the public sphere. Everyone else wrote sympathetically, and it was very heart-warming for me to hear people opening up to talk about what they lived through when someone close to them died. If I have learnt one thing from my own, personal experience of accompanying my father on the path towards his assisted death and staying with him while he was dying, it is this: it is high time for us all to reclaim death and to lead it back into life. We must free death from the taboos that still surround it.

This is therefore my most deeply felt advice: do start early with talking about death, long before you face the reality of death yourself. If possible, speak about death and dying, just as you talk about birth. Do mention that death involves pain, but that it sometimes also brings liberation. For these reasons, please give these momentous and life-changing events the importance they deserve.

April 2021

Today, you said it plainly: you have had enough. Not tired of life, just had enough. This is why you want to put an end to it, sooner rather than later. I know you – you won't be deterred. When one has had enough, whether with life or with food, it is the same; one doesn't want anymore. You will be ninety soon. I hope that you have, at least, enjoyed life.

I have known Father's attitude to people deciding to die ever since his sister opted to take her own life when she was ninety. Then, when my mobile rang, I was lost in the vast asphalted desert of an American supermarket car park. Father's voice was so spherically distorted that it sounded as if he was reading out a military bulletin. 'Sudden heart failure' he would have me believe. He dished up a story that was hard to credit and whose parts did not match up. It was our mother who, a few weeks later, enlightened us about the actual state of affairs. The half-truth was, in effect, one great big lie, and she was unwilling to leave it at that. Only then did Father talk to me and my brother Martin. Our aunt had departed this life helped by an assisted dying organisation. Father had stood by her, helping with the preparations and then held her hand when she accepted the potion from the 'angel of death'. He made no secret of the fact that he saw this as an option for himself. Mother wanted to hear nothing about it. She had always vehemently rejected suicide and disapproved of Father's intention 'to cut and run'.

That was the answer to your problems even then, wasn't it? The plan you had hatched with your favourite sister, should your lives not end the way you each wanted.

Two years later, my mother died of a brain tumour. Her illness caused her to lose her speech – but more than that: her mind. All channels of communication had broken off. She died just like a candle running out of oxygen. During the two months between diagnosis and death, in the days when she talked incoherently or not at all, our father, Martin and I had her fate in our hands. We had to decide according to the principles she had expressed when she could still talk: No to surgery, No to chemotherapy, Yes to death. As Mother had always distanced herself from assisted dying, it was clear, too, that going down that path was out of the question. But Father's position on this issue was absolutely certain and uncompromising. He would not want to die like this.

*

I saw you on the screen today, in 'Tagesschau'.[1] My God, it is hard to believe that you are ninety: you looked so young and fit the way you presented yourself to the audience. I take my hat off to you!

A prominent Swiss firm is celebrating its centenary. Father worked in this company for decades – first in accountancy, and then up the career ladder, rung by rung, until he reached the position of director general, as the top post was called in those days. He enjoys talking about those years and it is no coincidence that it is him, specifically, who is dragged in front of the camera by the TV crew to testify as 'witness of the times'. Father has the reputation of being a shrewd thinker and an eloquent speaker. No doubt the CEO also made a speech. But next to the grand old man he probably appeared bland. In this respect, he is not alone: he is but one of a long line of men who were overshadowed by Father, just like my brother and I were – it was impossible for us to stand out in his light.

---

[1] 'Tagesschau' is the name of the main news programme of the national Swiss TV station.

One of his favourite stories, which he loves to recount, was when he worked for a subsidiary of an American company, which dictated all of their market strategy from the New York headquarters. Father was not best pleased with this. When the CEO of the parent company arrived for a fleeting visit, Father picked him up from the airport, using the opportunity to teach him a lesson that was rather typical of him – cheeky and to the point. He covered up the front window on the driver's side with a newspaper, asked his boss to sit down on the passenger seat, placed himself behind the steering wheel and said, smiling: 'Now Bob, tell me how to drive.' The CEO declined. 'You see', Father chuckled, 'those who steer a car or run a firm must be able to decide on their own.' Yes, this is how Father became the important personality he was: with subtlety, wit and assertiveness he became one of the top managers in Switzerland.

Shortly before he retired, he played with the idea that it might be time for him to step into the second rank (further back was out of the question): 'As you get older you learn to turn into nothing again', he used to quote from one of his favourite poems. But today, in front of an audience and with cameras rolling, it is clear that my father is in his element standing at the front – preferably on the bridge. Second rank is not his thing. Today, he shows himself once more the way people love and admire him. Tomorrow, they will pester me about it, will rave about the old guy who is so full of energy and is such an admirable presence. Naturally, I shall agree.

In phases when he is overcome by self-criticism, when he is embarrassed by praise and glamour, he conjures up the image of the lighthouse whose bright beam shows the way to the sailors. And yet, it is dark at his feet. Father talks about the shadow clinging to every human being, accompanying everybody all through life.

Unfortunately, the shortcomings of distinguished people are often hidden because they are so brilliant. A few weaknesses would, I feel, be of benefit to them – it would somehow make them more human.

*

You have transferred ten thousand francs to Martin and to me. Thank you.

My gratitude and joy are mixed with a gloomy feeling. I cannot dispel the nagging thought that I am accepting charity. This is no accident. A few years before Mother died, Father signed over most of the family's assets to her as a gift, assuming he would die before her. This would ensure that, at the time the estate had to be divided if Father predeceased her, our mother would already own the estate, and her sons' compulsory legal share would be insignificant. After Mother's death, Father calculated on some scrap paper that each of his sons would receive twenty thousand francs. There was no mention of my brother Martin and me in Mother's will. Nowhere on the pages covered with Mother's small handwriting did we find our names. It seemed as if we had not existed in her life. Mother's last will and testament reflected entirely Father's and his financial adviser's ideas. The donations to Mother, so the will recorded, would revert to Father in the event Mother predeceased him. Swiss inheritance law complicated matters considerably. The fact that the sons were owed compulsory portions under the law could not be magically spirited away with a trick. This was not, however, what Martin and I were concerned about. We did not want to be treated like young, under-age children who could be slipped a coin every now and then.

You shook your head and harrumphed with indignation when we didn't keep the appointment with the land registry and refused to sign documents we did not comprehend. Wasn't it you who had always drummed into us that we must never sign anything we did not understand? Martin and I wanted to understand.

Why have you never talked to us about your income and our financial affairs? Were you worried we would evict Mother from her home? Were we still not adults in your eyes or were we too grown up? Your scheming woke us up – at last.

You had reckoned without fate. Mother died before you. You have strengthened my belief in life's uncertainties. There are matters you cannot influence.

Of course, we left the entirety of the fortune for Father to use. I cannot bear it when children, whatever their age, make demands on their parents' savings while they are still alive. On the other hand, however, the issue should have been raised and discussed.

I knew about the ten thousand francs and I also knew why he bestowed this sum on us: Father and I spent Christmas together in the mountains of the Grisons. He does not like to withdraw to what we consider our 'family fortress' on his own, because loneliness inevitably catches up with him there. Mother's presence can be felt in this second home more than anywhere else. Each picture, each window bay, each pot in its place – everything carries her own special stamp. It is there, in the mountains, that we talked about Mother, about living without her and about Father's feelings of having had enough. In these few days, I felt close to my father, until Tobias Stolte called; Father withdrew to his bedroom for the conversation with his financial advisor and friend – quite contrary to his normal manner.

Yes, I eavesdropped and heard what you said to him, that you would like to help your sons: one of them was, after all, divorced and had to support two families, and the other one was out of work. How right you are. Your magnanimity offends me because every franc of your money whispers: 'You clearly have not got a grip on your lives.' Let's be honest, Martin and I, we do not match up to your image of successful people; you would have liked to straighten out our life stories a bit.

It had taken far too long before I could separate myself from my father's view of the world and cut the umbilical cord, so to speak. Far too much was taken for granted: that we would go to university, that education was everything and that sport meant nothing, that the top was above and the bottom remained below – with the head ruling the gut. I felt guilty when I found my own role models and still continued to measure my successes against Father's value system. Unfortunately, my skills and achievements were reflected in those spheres of life that my father considered senseless and useless. Self-doubt was my constant companion.

The liberation from Father's way of looking at things and from his standards hit me unexpectedly. The moment came in the middle of the jungle between Panama and Colombia. I was twenty-six and had assembled a three-man expedition, fiercely determined to cross the 'Darién Gap', a 200km-wide dense swathe of forest, attempting to travel over land from Panama City to Colombia, with an off-road vehicle. A one-hundred strong British elite unit had succeeded six years earlier, but nobody else had. The

Panamanian authorities cautioned us in the strongest possible terms, the Swiss consul urgently advised against, and the US army categorically ruled out any rescue mission in case of an emergency. The words of warning missed the target: on the contrary, they had the effect of accelerating the fire I carried within me.

There I was, on the 31st day of my recklessness, high up on a 100m steep escarpment called 'Devil's Switchback', weighing in at a mere 52kg and with a broken leg. Weakened by days of diarrhoea, every move was torture. My brain worked slowly, but my thoughts were mercilessly clear: either we managed to get our vehicle down into this gorge, across the shallow stream and then up the bush-covered embankment on the other side, or I could pack the necessities and return home. Staring down the steep slope, my pulse pounding in my broken leg, and being uncomfortably aware of the sound of the winch with its steel cable, taut to breaking point, I suddenly realised: I can do it! He cannot do this! Never would Father be able to master this extreme situation. His whole classical education would not save him from perishing here. In the jungle, battling against the adversities of engineering and nature, I was way ahead of him. Hardly able to keep upright, it dawned on me how wrong I had been for all those years: instead of challenging his norms and values, I had always questioned myself.

Do you remember that I gave you my diary to read afterwards? You read it and thanked me politely. But you had not registered the momentousness – my life remained strange and unfamiliar to you. A couple of years ago you confessed to me over lunch that you had not really been able to appreciate my achievement at that time. Only much later did you comprehend just how important those days had been for me. That made me feel good. If it had been said earlier, it would have been even better.

*

Yesterday, Martin, his wife Denise and their son Tim came to dinner with Angela and me. My grown-up sons Mathias and Fabian were also there. Since our separation, I don't see the two of them that often, but our relationship has remained intact.

Mathias, Fabian and Tim watch a DVD of the Hollywood movie *Troy*. Father would like it; he loves battles, above all epic Greek tales of heroes, but he does not care for the cinema: too noisy, too much irrelevant stuff. His learning springs from books; that is his world.

We are having coffee and we talk – obviously about Father. The conversation brings relief and comforts me. I now see his gesture of giving me ten thousand francs in a different light. The action certainly also shows care and concern. Nevertheless, my fury remains, because his 'obol'[2] (as he would put it) makes me ashamed too.

Denise reckons that reviewing our lives is distorting our perspective. She believes that our assessment of Father's current actions is too much influenced by our childhood memories. As sons, we must not underestimate our mother's role when we now talk about any aspect of our father's life. She had never prevented Father from acting like the dominant force he was. In Denise's view, her addiction to shopping reflected something like displacement activity for something that she could not receive. Denise is right: the carefully erected memorials to childhood and youth obstruct my view of the father who presents himself today. I find it hard to see, and to accept,

---

[2] An 'obolos' is an ancient Greek coin. To call ten thousand francs an 'obol' implies that his father considers the sum a small donation.

the change he has undergone. He wrote a very beautiful letter to Martin on his birthday, and Denise thinks my brother should save it, because she believes these words could overturn Martin's fixed image of his father.

Occasionally, Father also reviews his past.

What are you thinking about when you cast your mind back? Are you merely wandering through all the pictures of your life, satisfied with the exhibits in the showrooms, or do you actually venture down into the basement looking for what's missing? Do you come across pieces of your collection that you are reluctant to open up to the public? Does your eye suddenly glimpse sketches and images that should not have come into existence, of which you are ashamed?

Angela and I have been invited to dinner with Father. This is a first, as it introduces new members of the family to each other: me with Angela, my new partner, and him with his companion Bettina and her grown-up daughters. It is a lovely evening; we understand each other well, and there is no sign of Father being fed up with life. He throws anecdotes around as usual and regales us with jokes that have not amused me for ages. If you get the punchline after three words, laughing seems a waste of time, and the uninitiated must consider us entirely lacking any sense of humour. More recently, I have noticed his voice crack over certain poetic quotations as his emotions overwhelm him. He shrugs off such feelings as senile whining, which is something he cannot bear. At such moments, Father feels strange to me; I cannot deal with these rarely displayed splinters of emotion. I would love to take over his pieces, add mine to his and make them all into one picture. I hardly ever do it, because he finds it embarrassing. And so do I, when all is said and done.

Father is especially fond of bons mots when he uses them to animate dinner parties. They, in particular, bestow on him this much-praised, urbane charm. But why do I always forget the details so quickly? Am I not listening anymore or is it my bad memory? Take this evening: something about women and how they have their price. It was really funny and I thought of my mother's shopping addiction. That was it, as far as that joke being amusing was concerned.

*

You have scarcely talked about dying recently. This is a good thing. The prospect of your death has been taking up too much time in my life. I have not even been able to process Mother's death – it happened so fast. Hold on, please, stay active, add another chapter to your life, even if you do feel it already too long.

A few days ago, I read Dieter Wellershoff's autobiographical book *Blick auf einen fernen Berg*.[3] The author describes how his younger brother dies of leukaemia. And now I sit at my desk, churned up from watching Susanne Bier's film *After the wedding*. Everything in this Danish film revolves around the protagonist dying of cancer. Scenes when he tries to ignore the illness alternate with scenes of sheer rage over his fate. Not wishing – or not able – to talk about it, suffering from intense physical pain and from the wounds that were inflicted on the life of his soul. We observe rearing up and crumpling, friends and family confronted with helplessness and hopelessness. Is all of this in store for me, or will it be different because Father chooses his death freely?

---

[3] The title means 'View of a distant mountain' (not available in English in 2020).

What happened in Mother's case? I realise that I have not thought enough about her dying. It has been five years this week. What role did I play, who has allocated which part to me and what have I chosen myself? Have I correctly interpreted Mother's confused utterances? Was I with her when she needed me? Was I close to her?

I remember that depressing drive. Mother had secured an appointment at short notice for surgery on her tumour. Our parents had to cut short their holidays in the mountains at once if they didn't want to miss that chance. Father asked me to drive them both back in Mother's new car. He had not been driving for some years, and Mother, who had sat behind the wheel but a few days ago, was now no longer able to. Father appeared helpless and exhausted, Mother was furious and irritable. She talked in an agitated way; sometimes her sentences were intelligible, but mostly they made no sense. She made it clear in no uncertain terms that she did not like that hospital and would only stay there if she could have a single room. Father was confident that that could be arranged. We were mostly silent on the way to Zurich. Mother no longer wished to talk to Father, and I did not dare to address Mother for fear of not understanding her answers, which would have irritated her even more. As we reached Rapperswil – not far from home – the phone rang in the car. Mother waved her arms about and shook her head to indicate that she did not want to take the call. I did not succeed in silencing the device: we remained at the mercy of the loud ringing.

It was Friday, and Mother was supposed to be in hospital by 6 p.m. because no admissions could be processed after that. There was just about time for a quick stopover at home to leave the holiday wardrobe and collect the necessary stuff for hospital. Mother's rage knew no bounds. Father's rush seemed unfair and lacking in dignity to her. She stood in the bathroom and tipped the entire content of her cosmetics bag on to the floor. She rejected all help.

An hour later, we sat at a small wooden table on the third floor of the hospital. Patients dragged themselves down the long linoleum-covered corridors past us and nurses scurried from room to room. But nobody seemed to be responsible for looking after Mother. One nurse said that there was no vacant single room for Mother. She wanted to return home. Father negotiated; he agreed to accept a room for emergencies, on the condition that it would have to be vacated if an emergency occurred during the night. The hospital was, after all, a place for acute care, the nurse said.

More MRI scans of Mother's brain were taken at the weekend. The tumour had grown drastically and had metastasised. On Monday, the doctor told us, i.e. Father, Martin and me, that it was possible to operate, but that a cure was improbable. The decision was ours. We wanted to have a discussion with Mother, of course. At least we hoped that she would understand what we had to tell her. I was the one chosen to speak, as we felt that, of the three of us, I was best placed to interpret our mother's words in those days. Together, we sat ourselves at her bedside. I had never delivered a death sentence before. I felt utterly miserable and wretched. However one begins, what words one chooses, the message at the end is always the same: you will die. Mother appeared to understand it all; she was quiet, as if she had already known. And this was quite possibly the case. After the chemotherapy following her earlier leukaemia diagnosis, she once said that she never wanted to undergo that again. The question was whether we should assume that this was still the case or whether she had changed her mind in the meantime and wanted to do everything in her power to stay alive. None of us could understand what Mother meant when she responded. If only she had been able to express a single clear thought: 'Yes, I would like to' or 'No, I do not want to continue'! She could merely shake her head, however, and we were at a loss to know what that referred to.

One morning, I found her crying in her hospital bed. It was only the second time in my life that I had seen my mother in tears. I sat down next to her and tried to suffer the sorrow with her – in silence. At one point she sat up, gestured towards the window with her hand, and called out: 'But surely not like that!' I didn't know whether to look for what she meant in front of or behind the windowpane. Another time she stood in front of the mirror and tried to comb her hair, holding the brush the wrong way round. Shortly afterwards, she fell silent and turned to the wall. Being silent does not mean that she does not want to hear anything, I thought. I played some soft music on the CD player I had brought along, hoping Mother still had access to music.

The hospital needed the room again. They did not have enough rooms and nobody knew how long Mother would live. They were not equipped to treat patients in need of long-term care. Ten days before she died, Father found a beautiful room in a nearby nursing home. We brought a small sofa and a little table from home, as well as a few personal items, and hoped that Mother would feel comfortable. She sat in her armchair just once, looked out of the window and said: 'Beautiful.' After that her eyes were almost always closed and she was silent.

There was scarcely any physical contact in our mother–child relationship. At least I cannot remember being hugged as boys or teenagers when we were sad. When I had a nightmare and wanted to get into my parents' bed, I found no shelter there. Mother once explained to me later that parenting experts had advised against such methods in those days, and this rule was strictly enforced by my parents. Comfort was always conveyed through words.

I did not know now whether Mother liked having her hand held or her sweaty forehead stroked. I didn't dare take her in my arms: we had never done that. I hoped she would feel that I was close when we listened to music together.

Mother died during the night. The evening before, the nurse had felt her skin and said to Father: 'She may well die tonight.' Father decided to spend the night in her room. An additional bed was put into the room and he went to sleep at eleven o'clock. When he approached Mother's bed at two o'clock, she had stopped breathing.

*

Checking family finances. Father and Tobias Stolte summoned Martin and me to a semi-official look at the 'current state of financial circumstances'. Tobias Stolte has been Father's financial adviser for decades. They had met when they did military service together. Stolte had asked Father how he invested his income. Not only had a business relationship developed, but the two became friends.

My brother had initiated the meeting in Father's city office, with its massive director's desk from his time as CEO in a dominating position and its walls decorated with historical engravings and military paraphernalia. Up to that time, I must remind myself, we had been denied a glimpse of Father's accounts. When the estate was divided after Mother's death, the two old men concealed quite a lot – be it intentionally or because they had exercised discretion for decades when it came to financial affairs. The thought that our family might be wealthy struck me for the first time when I was about twenty and my parents were on holiday; I came upon evidence indicating that my mother's new diamond ring had a value of around sFr. 80,000. Mother wore the ring only for special occasions (in later years there was a copy of the original which, as recommended by the insurance company, spent a rather miserable existence in a safe in the bank). I am not sure any more now whether my memory is correct. Perhaps there was one zero less? I shall – if the piece still reposes in the safe – find out after Father's death. At that time it became clear: my parents are rich. 'Rich', however, was not a word one was allowed to say in Father's presence. 'We are not rich; we are well off', he corrected.

Today, then, we are to be granted a virtual glance into the treasure chest. However, following unctuous introductory words by the owner, we merely get a list of the accumulation of costs relating to the three existing properties. Those of us without properties reacted with amazement, all the more so when Tobias Stolte declares that the annual running costs for the properties could be easily covered through uncommitted funds. Uncommitted funds – there was money to spare? This had never been mentioned before; and this time, too, they were apparently not worth mentioning.

Martin and I reacted with unease and later also with resentment. Why this restraint, why the falling back into the old pattern of the all-powerful father and the immature offspring? Those without possessions demand clarification, while he who possesses everything darts querying glances in the direction of his financial adviser, who returns them to the sender at once. At last, we have Father's agreement to put his cards on the table: 'We are, after all, grown up people.'

Father and Stolte seem rattled, Martin and I are irritated, and we are all suddenly uncertain whether the flat in which Father currently lives was recorded as belonging to all heirs after Mother's death, or whether it is merely noted in the land register as a security against our future claim. What heroes we are! We do not talk openly about money and we do not talk openly about death. As if we had a lot of time to do so.

Tobias Stolte urges us not to wait until April for a valuation of the material assets by one of Sotheby's experts, but to find a date in March if possible. Why the hurry? I am starting to sort the remarks, which could be taken to refer to Father's death, into a timeline. I suspect that the activities surrounding his 90th birthday in May are merely diversionary manoeuvres (what he would call 'decoy tactics') so that his death before that date cannot be interpreted as intentional. He also says, though, that everyone in his family died between 90 and 92. Father is a great believer in traditions.

After the official part of the meeting, Father treats us to lunch at a nearby restaurant. We turn from the 'haves' and the 'have-nots' into four human beings with their own opinions. That is certainly an improvement. Tobias Stolte suggests that Martin and I should be on first-name terms with him. Has he offered this privilege to us as people or just to the future heirs to the estate?

Then we part ways. Father, a slightly hunched old man, carefully puts one foot in front of the other. I know that he would like to march upright, striding briskly, towards his destination. Today, however, his destination is no longer the management of a company ready for acquisition, but his ear specialist. At a door no more than fifty steps ahead of me, he brings his head very close to the lettering on the name plate – his eyes are no longer what they once were, either. He pushes hard against the doorway and is swallowed up by the dark entrance. I admire him for his reasoning power, his charm and his near-inexhaustible knowledge, and that there is a vulnerable side to him I find endearing. And yet, when I think of the way he patronises me, this silent rage torments me again.

Are there other issues, apart from asset values, that we should discuss now? We don't have much time. You are not leaving us much time.

*

I believed you to be stable and in good shape. On the telephone this morning, however, I have felt that you are not. Has that weariness with life got hold of you again?

Sunday morning is an unusual time for a phone call from Father. It has to be something urgent, something that leaves him no peace. It is the question of how to celebrate his birthday. For months he has been dithering between a last big party or an enjoyable slap-up meal with close family. But what do we mean by 'close family'? The situation is

31

no longer as straightforward as it had once been. He worries about friends who had invited him to lavish birthday parties and who might therefore expect his hospitality in return. This morning he decided to go for an open house reception. Let those come who really want to see him. But now he has started to agonise over the actual planning. What if too many people turn up at the same time? Would it not be better if Bettina were there, too, as she and Angela or Denise could perhaps look after the women? But his partner does not wish to do this: she does not feel comfortable with Father's circle of friends. I am the same – his natural habitat is not our world. He accepts this, but it makes him sad, because something is not going his way. He appears never to have asked himself whether *he* would like to live among people who are very different; for example, in a community of football fans. 'No, definitely not', he answers, adding that he was glad to have had the chance to get to know the life of farmers, of soldiers and that of factory workers.

At times like this I would like to stop being gentle and shout loudly: 'Wake up, please wake up at last! Try to see the world through other people's eyes, not only your own.' Instead, I urge him, restrained as I have been brought up to be, that it is not enough to *know* the worries of these people in order to *feel* the way they actually live. He concedes that I might be right and that he would never have liked to live like a farmer. Endorsement of my view, then, but that won't change his mind. He is far too certain that he is correct.

On this Sunday morning I succeed in calming my father: we shall face this together, the father with his sons. In recent weeks I have cherished the hope that he might still take pleasure from some aspects of his life. But life is not playing along. He claims to be tired of being seen as the ever eloquent, quick-witted, energetic man he no longer believes himself to be. Sooner or later, we are all punished for the roles we so eagerly played, even when they did not really suit us.

Father has again succumbed to an age-related depression. He does not like to hear that word. In his view, depressions afflict people who do not have a grip on themselves, and that is something he has never accepted for himself.

*

I have browsed through one of Father's books of poems over the last few days and have found the emotions he hides so well in his daily routine. Father writes because he enjoys poetry. When he has penned a few poems, he gets them printed and bound – the ones I have in my hands right now have a blue linen jacket and are dedicated to my mother, 'who has contributed to what follows in many conversations and with thought-provoking suggestions', as he puts it in the preface.

Did you really listen to her? Or did you just take what suited your thoughts from her words?

Father gave this blue collection of poems to Mother for Christmas, her last one. She had locked herself into the bedroom, struck down by the tumour. She did not share her bitterness and sadness with anyone. Least of all with Father.

*

Again, Father allows us to have a share of his material fortune.

The money has arrived. Thank you. It will be very useful: the tax bill must be paid, my divorce will cost, too, and one of your grandsons still needs my financial support. You tell me that, for the first time in your life, you earned just by being there. You have brought the seller and the buyer of a property together, and for this transaction you are due an agent's commission, which you want to share with Martin and me. This is a generous gesture – even if it shows, once again, who among us is the superstar. It's a good life, being in your shadow.

Father's policy, when it came to pocket money, was logical, fair and consistent. As school children, we had 50 centimes per week to spend as we liked. In the autumn, my brother and I were always made to rake leaves in the garden. This added another 50 centimes per hour. I had a small plastic tube into which my 50-centime coins fitted precisely. Colourful icons were stuck on the sides of this 'piggy bank' – depicting rain and thunderstorms at the bottom, in the middle a cloud with the sun peeking out and, on the top, the face of a laughing sun. That's where I aimed to go with my hard-earned coins.

As a teenager, I received money to manage myself. I had an accounts book, where I had to list all expenses in detail. When the money was spent, I got more. Admittedly, only expenses necessary for subsistence were accepted, such as meals away from home, bus and train fares, or schoolbooks. Entertainment, such as magazines or visits to the cinema, had to be paid out of our pocket money, which had been increased in the meantime.

When I was sixteen, I asked my father if he would buy me a moped to get to school. He did not feel this was necessary as, in his view, the bus service was excellent. I therefore bought the moped from my savings, but kept listing the cost of the bus tickets, including every increase in the charges. Father accepted this ruse without further ado, smiling to himself.

*

See! Together we got through it yesterday; together we celebrated your ninetieth birthday with an open house reception. Your friends from the Rotary Club came, as well as a few old colleagues and business associates. I did miss personal friends from your private life; I only spotted one.

I do not know who Father's best friend is. I have never seen friends from his school and university times. We never spontaneously visited anyone at the weekend and if any visitors showed up unexpectedly at our house, my mother reacted with panic. We were told to keep completely silent and the door was not to be opened if anyone rang the bell. That was fine with both of them. My mother hated to play hostess without preparation – her perfectionism did not permit spontaneous hospitality. And my father wanted to use weekends to work on his papers or to write speeches and books. Occasionally, one of Father's business connections turned into a close companionship. Personal worries were, however, never discussed; private problems had to stay within the confines of the family. If there were close friends, I do not know them.

Everything turned out as planned; a constant coming and going, all in a controlled manner and manageable. You sparkled on your birthday and were admired; people like and adore you.

There was only one thing I did not like about this day: Father had invited Konrad Eschner, a friend of the same age. They had not seen each other for a long time. At Konrad Eschner's 80th birthday they agreed to celebrate the 90th together, with a glittering party. Konrad Eschner, suffering from a curvature of the spine, walks with a stick.

He had travelled by train, and at the station he had had to wait for a taxi for more than an hour – in the rain. Now he is standing outside the door, bent over and exhausted. His condition disturbs my father; Eschner does not fit in his circle of radiant Rotary members. Chairs would have to be moved, people would have to get up to clear some space, and small talk would be interrupted in an embarrassing way. My father instructs me to sit Konrad Eschner with a different group of guests. Rather reluctantly, it seems to me, Father joins him for a few minutes. After that, he gratefully leaves his one-time comrade-in-arms to his sons and turns back to his illustrious guests.

Am I doing you a disservice? You know, I am only trying to shed light onto the shadow at the bottom of the lighthouse showing your human weaknesses. You do not have to worry; they won't diminish your glow.

Even though Konrad Eschner had travelled for more than two hours, he set off again after 30 minutes. Nothing had come of the glittering party for him, not even a 'do you remember' story with my father.

I am furious. When I was a child, you always explained to me how to help a blind person across the road in a considerate way. I should not ask: 'Shall I help you across the road?' The correct phrase was: 'May I accompany you across the road?'

While my rage subsides, I can guess my father's reaction. His party had been disturbed by an unexpected item on the programme. Konrad Eschner had come to the party in a way Father himself would wish to avoid at all costs: disabled and in a pitiful state. He has changed from a former companion into a nuisance.

When guests ask after my brother's occupation, my father answers that he has just retired. This is sugar-coating of the first order, learnt and practised in these circles for decades. Martin has recently been dismissed and now looks after his child and the household. Full stop. My brother declares himself to be a house husband, thus paraphrasing exactly the division of work in his family. But 'has retired' sounds much more innocuous, fits better into a successful biography. Father cannot understand Martin's anger. He does not comprehend that this avoidance of the truth only demeans what Martin is – a really good father and house husband. Inadvertently, Father reveals his true attitude: house husbands are failures – his son is a failure. Old wounds are opened up.

Father tells those who wish him many more years of health and happiness, when they say goodbye, that he hopes to be spared that. This coquettish acknowledgement of his own age delights his guests. The truth about his state of mind and about his plans – the 'whole truth', 'nothing but the truth', a maxim from the legal world, which Father liked to quote – goes for nothing, yet again.

In the evening, Father is exhausted and visibly marked by the strains of the day: from ten o'clock in the morning to eight o'clock in the evening he has played the attentive host and man of the world without pause. The guests have confirmed time and again how they admired my father's mental presence. The birthday party had, however, exceeded his physical powers.

*

The following day, I put Father's birthday letters in order and arrange the presents he received. He has asked me to help. Despite his exhaustion, he urges me impatiently to do this at once. His wishes, phrased as favours, are usually demands. There is no hurry, he adds, only to contradict himself by calling me – at increasingly short intervals – to ensure that his order is being dealt with speedily. My father is proud of his impatience. Apparently, a businessman once told him that he accomplished his goals only with patience. Father's response was that he could not understand this: he owed his success primarily to his impatience.

The well-wishers have made an effort and sent handwritten notes and letters. This is hard for my father. While he is delighted to receive well-intentioned recognition and appreciates the special touch of letters penned in longhand, he is annoyed because he finds deciphering handwriting even more difficult than small print. I read the letters to him and note down in thick red felt pen the name of the sender, whether there was a present included, and whether Father plans to answer by telephone or letter. Ever since writing – which had always given him such great pleasure – has become torture, he prefers to phone. Nowadays, he brushes aside all the admiration for his person, expressed in these cards and letters. Reluctantly, he acknowledges wishes for a continued long life. He does not want to hear anything that might make the big decision more difficult. The book of life is to be closed.

My father supported many people with help and advice. He also helped young people financially when he felt they deserved assistance and if anyone worried that they could not repay their debt, Father would smile and say that would not be necessary; his assistance was a form of generation aid. He only expected that the same type of support would be passed onto some other young people when that was possible. This is a good model and quite a few well-wishers mention gratefully that Father had helped them in this way.

*

What you tell us makes us believe that you have been dragging yourself from one high point to the next since your birthday. These are the happy events of your life, which keep you from dying. You will allow me to talk about 'high points' I am sure. You have, after all, reserved the 'milestones' for the really big events of your life. Coming from the second rank, it has become difficult to achieve milestones.

Spending the Whitsun weekend in Bad Ragaz with Bettina, the carefully prepared speech entitled 'Prägung und Wandel'[4] in front of your influential friends in the Club, and the enjoyable rehab week in the clinic Schloss Mammern[5] – those are experiences I would list under 'high points'.

Father tries to escape the drab monotony of a pensioner's life – not enough challenges. His doctor sent him to the clinic in Mammern because he suffered from dizziness. He had been there twice, but he cannot remember it well. The first stay he wrongly believes to have taken place much earlier, at the time when, forty-five years ago, he suffered from bleeding in the stomach. In fact, both stays actually happened only a few years ago. Each time the death of a loved one had thrown him off course.

I remember well the days seven years ago: on my return from the USA I discovered that my father was but a shadow of himself. He could not concentrate, was mentally

---

[4] This can be roughly translated as 'Cultural imprint and social transformation'.
[5] Both Bad Ragaz and Mammern have world-class rehabilitation clinics.

confused and had literally collapsed into himself. His favourite sister's death had affected him badly. He was, however, in denial – claiming that it was only the physical exertion of it all: he had to clear his sister's apartment in record time, prepare her funeral, deal with the estate. It was all too much for him. My mother, who had herself only just recovered from leukaemia, was not to be fooled. She knew about Father's deep bond with his older sister, was aware of the role he played in her assisted death, and had personal experience of how suppressed feelings could be reflected in physical symptoms. My father seemed suddenly to have aged by a decade. Mother tried to stop him driving because he had become a danger to himself and others. Fines accumulated and a colleague reported that Father had overlooked him on a pedestrian crossing. Mother appealed to me to talk to Father.

Ever since my childhood my parents used me as a mediator. The reason for this was probably my position in the family: I was the youngest, a shy child, anxious for harmony. Occasionally, Father asked me to convince Mother of something, then both requested that I appeal to Martin, or Mother attempted, with my support, to win over Father for a plan she had. I found this normal; it gave me the feeling that I was needed. I would never use my own sons as family mediators.

On a hot summer's day, my mother and I took Father to a nice restaurant on the lake. My father's bent posture as he walked along, the bright yellow sun umbrellas, the white-covered tables and the waiters in livery – the picture is clearly etched in my memory. I knew that this conversation was important and I feared failure. Father should bear in mind that he could destroy his image – which he had built up over a life-time – in seconds, if he ran someone over. Nobody would talk of the great strategist and clever thinker anymore; people would only pity him and remember the woeful fall from grace and his irresponsible act. Father listened silently. Next day he handed over his car key and booked himself in for a three-week course of treatment in Mammern. It seemed to me that, for the first time ever, I had had an impact on my father's life. He calmed down in the clinic, found time to process his sister's death and returned full of optimism and thirst for action.

Two years later, he returned to Mammern after Mother's death. This time, too, he had tried to sit out his grief by keeping control and remaining rational – a typical reaction for my parents. As before, the repressed emotions exhibited themselves in the form of physical malfunction. My parents have passed onto me the inability to show pain, let alone any inner storms, believing that this was a manifestation of dignity.

And today, I drive Father to Mammern for the third time. He is in good spirits and full of hope that his stay would give him a new lease of life again. We chat in a relaxed way over lunch. Father is interested in my partnership with Angela and in my professional prospects, which are darkening. He talks openly about worries over his physical breakdown, but also about a book project that he wants to realise after his return. I am trying to enthuse him for audio books and new technology in the field of reading aids, and I offer my help with future plans. We are there for each other.

I can still feel this closeness, even though I cannot remember the exact words we exchanged. We were both grateful that the other was there and for the support we granted each other. In the past, my father had looked after me. Nowadays, the care flows in the other direction. It is as if water were flowing uphill. This does not fit into the familiar scene. I have to rethink.

May I accompany you across the road?

When we say goodbye, Father slips me some petrol money for 'my good offices', but this time I am not ashamed: today his gesture expresses gratitude.

The days in Mammern do not go as Father desired: early mornings start with taking blood pressure and he is forced to follow a different rhythm; it is now silence, not he, who reigns. Nothing in the daily routine is different from previous stays, except that Father is not the same. This time he sees the 'decrepit' patients with other eyes: he belongs to them now. He is loath to establish contact and this throws him back onto himself. With each new day, his loneliness grows. He goes home early.

*

For about ten years, there has always been a get-together for Uncle Hans's birthday – to cultivate the family spirit, so to speak. This tradition had only started after the death

47

of Aunt Therese, Uncle Hans's late wife. Perhaps this was the first time that members of the family had become aware of the transience of life and the need for such social gatherings.

On the drive there, my father tells me that he believes he is losing his mind. He reports having sent two letters the day before yesterday but cannot remember, with the best will in the world, to whom he had written one of them. I try to calm him down, explaining that not remembering is not the same as losing one's mind. Old people's memories can no longer absorb and recall new information so well. That, together with his quick-witted and astute exchanges in discussions, surely means that there is no cause for concern.

The location and time of the family party are the same every year, but the faces change. Quarrelling, separations and deaths have thinned the ranks. New faces from the extended circle have filled any gaps, as if it were a game about outwitting mortality. Father is not comfortable between the overly pious, frail Aunt Berta and Uncle Hans, who talks politics at the top of his voice. He increasingly avoids such gatherings. School reunions, as well: while they had in the past presented a stage for showing off achievements and success, they have now gained a gloomy aspect. Hardly anyone remained and he was soon going to be the only one there, my father reckons. And he did not need a reunion simply to talk to himself. He finds the breakup of his generation demoralising, because it mirrors his own decay. On the way back from Uncle Hans's birthday party, my father admits grumpily to having been bored. Perhaps his thoughts hurry ahead to the next day. . .

Are you already thinking of the farewell dinner with Martin, who is flying to Nepal for four years on Wednesday? Are you thinking what we are all thinking? Perhaps tomorrow will be the last time that you look into each other's eyes.

Last week, Father reassured me that he would not be as weepy as his father when he had to go abroad for a long period. My father loves heroes and avoids sissies. Men who show their emotions are categorised as sissies. On Sunday, Martin and Tim, Angela, Father and I therefore sit at lunch in the Restaurant Sternen – in an orderly and civilised manner – and we talk as if there were a tomorrow and a day after tomorrow. Father pulls a gold-plated pen out of a small bag and gives it to my brother as a present. It is the pen with which he wrote many of his manuscripts and speeches: it should accompany him on his travels. I am touched. Here is the spark of warmth I had wished for. His pen. I do not know whether Martin understands the meaning of this gesture: Father's pen is an integral part of him.

We eat, we talk. We fold our napkins, reach for our jackets and coats, say goodbye to the landlord, as if it were a day like every other. We take a few steps along the lake, a few of pictures with our mobiles and exchange a few words, carefully avoiding moments of sentimental silence.

There is a man of about thirty-five on a park bench; next to him is a sports bag and an open can of beer. He has been observing us for a while and we have exchanged glances. When we pass his bench, he addresses us:

'What a nice party. Are you celebrating a birthday?'

'No, it's a farewell.'

'Ah! Yes, that must be hard.'

In our family there are no touching goodbyes. One does not wish to be touched in these cases, literally. This is a family tradition. It will be the same today.

*

That evening, I wanted to write down every detail of the farewell, so as not to leave anything to the mercy of oblivion. I grappled for words, started typing – only to erase it all again at once, individual letters and characters. I mulled over this parting for days, again and again. But instead of being able to work with a wealth of images scooped from a vast lake, I found only a gaping black hole inside myself.

Having to watch Martin and you saying goodbye rendered me speechless at that time.

The memory has returned. After the walk along the lake, we drive Father home. There, at the garage door, the two passengers get out, one of them frail, but carefully holding his posture, the other biding his time and unable to take the initiative. I hope that they can embrace each other – a last time, probably one last time. But they do not. A formal manly handshake, a couple of affectionate words – perhaps this is more genuine. You cannot undo through an embrace what has been weighing on the soul for years. One ought to have talked about it. First about the wounds, mutually inflicted, about the desire to understand the other, and then they could have silently hugged each other, a form of present, so to speak.

Father shuffles to the blind corner of the driveway to warn us of oncoming cars. He waves us through with brisk, forceful movements to make sure we can join the traffic. When we are level, he raises his hand to salute us. We drive for a while, lost in our thoughts. Then Martin says to Tim: 'Strange, isn't it?'

*

During the last few weeks, I have tried to remember the dim and distant past. How did we live as a family – Father, Mother, my brother and me? I looked for pictures from my childhood to embed into my present life. I did not succeed the way I had wanted to. I only found fragments.

How was it at that time? Did you cradle us in your arms when we were babies? Did you cuddle us, or was this stuff for mothers? I would love to ask you, but you recently said that you don't like looking into the past. Who else can I ask?

I remember that we always went on a little Swiss excursion over Whitsun. Father drove us to places that would broaden our horizons. We visited palaces and castles, and he brought the battles between the Habsburgs and the Swiss confederates back to life for us, just like his father had done for him. He explained how churches and cathedrals were built, how to recognise whether a colonnade was Gothic, Doric or Ionic, or why mountain ranges organised themselves into folds. He knew which word had a Greek or a Latin origin, why the wheel was the greatest invention of mankind and why Hannibal crossed the Alps. At the beginning, these outings were varied and fun, but later, the ever-increasing traffic and the congestion on public holidays led to tensions. Too much time was wasted on the road.

As for the Sunday picnics: we drove to the edge of a wood or a clearing. Father first unpacked the big heavy deckchair for Mother, then the woollen blanket and the picnic hamper with the plastic plates, napkins, cutlery and the thermos. I particularly liked this large box, which was fire-engine red and had shiny locks. Being boys, we went to look for wood and then lit a fire with our father, while Mother dished out rice or potato salad and skinned the cervelats so that we could grill them, skewered on the hazelnut twigs we had cut and prepared for this purpose beforehand. Father showed us how to make incisions in the sausages to ensure they did not burst over the fire.

Later, while Mother was absorbed in a woman's magazine, Father cut some pine bark from the tree trunk and taught us to carve small wooden boats. I loved nothing better, though, than finding a small stream where we could build a dam, or channel the trickle of water in the nearly dried-out bed into ever-changing directions.

Do you remember how, as a dare, we swam out to the big rock in the icy water of the River Maggia? Or how, near our holiday home, we broke stones to construct a little wall and how we then cemented it? For posterity, we bricked in a memorial coin. This felt immensely significant to me. I was happy.

Later on, Sundays became more challenging: Father was increasingly absorbed by work and had to devote his weekends to reading files. There was just about enough time for eating out and for a Sunday walk, which bored Martin and me. On one occasion, this coincided with a football game between Switzerland and Sweden in Berlin; a decider over who would make it to the world cup in Chile and, for us boys, it was the game of the century. How we would have loved to listen to the radio, but we had to go on the Sunday walk. No excuse. After we had got back home, Martin and I ran to the radio and listened to the reporter's voice – he was commenting on the last 15 minutes. Martin could not bear the tension and locked himself into the bathroom five minutes before the end of the game.

As puberty set in, my father became ever more distant to me. He lived in another world. At that time, he was often away in the evening and at weekends, and when he was at home, we mostly saw each other over dinner or he helped me with Latin and French vocabulary. He appeared not to be aware of my real problems; in any case, he never asked me about them and I never discussed them with him. Once, around ten o'clock in the evening, all my accumulated frustrations erupted with a violence I had never known. I was about sixteen then. I believe he had forbidden me to go to a rock concert at the weekend and I had tried to convince him how important it was for me to be there. He argued objectively and cogently, but he did not understand me. We stood in my parents' salmon-coloured bathroom together and I screamed at him that he did not understand me, could not understand me, and would never be in a position to understand me, as he was never at home anyway. I was shaking all over, tears running down my cheeks. Since then, I have only ever cried once more in my life. Father wanted to say something, but I rushed out of the house and hurried around the nearby pond in the pitch-dark night. The depth of the water reached for me enticingly.

Father tried his best over the following weeks, but there was no way we could get close to each other again. Our worlds remained separated.

*

For just over six months or so, Father has fluctuated between phases of depression and powerful, confident appearances. The latter result in everyone praising him. One such appearance was only last week. Just like a beacon, he sent out rays of light.

I was pleased for him, proud of him and also exasperated. The following day he falls back into his loneliness again – the feeling that he has 'had enough'. Since Mother's death, since he has constantly been in the grip of frailty, Father has had these two faces. Most people only see his radiant side.

You should allow people to participate in your dark days; that would do you good. Stop being a memorial – do become a man of flesh and blood.

Hope and thirst for action are followed by exhaustion and resignation. It is as if my father could not decide where he belongs. The ups and downs of the recent months wear me out. No sooner have I adapted to a phase than it is overturned and replaced by a new one. My memories of these weeks are fleeting and colourless, revealing only silhouettes. This is what I obviously have to cling to now: shadows.

*

One evening in the autumn, Father and I sit in the Restaurant Hirschen. Over coffee he mentions it yet again, and he comes straight to the point. He intends to take his own life.

Why don't you just do it, at long last?

Let me guess: you still have a few big plans. You are afraid that dying hurts; you have never been a brave patient. You feel an obligation towards Bettina. You do not want to be responsible for the sorrow you cause others through your voluntary death. You fear for your good reputation. You hope that death will, after all, come for you. Which is it?

While he is on his morning walk on a cool late autumn day, Father has a fall. He calls me from the Accident and Emergency department of the hospital to tell me about it, saying that he could not remember the fall, that he had been on the way back home and alone. He had been bleeding from the back of his head and unable to get up by himself. A neighbour had seen him lying on the pavement and the caretaker had driven him to hospital. Father had neither ID nor money on him: he had only wanted to go for a short walk.

These days are difficult for me: there are problems with my line manager, who takes all the pleasure out of my work. I have my ears to the ground and am looking for a new job. Around lunch time, I have an appointment with a potential new employer. Just emerging from a tough business meeting in my current firm, my mind is already on the upcoming job interview. My father calls from the hospital, reports on what has happened and asks me to bring him fresh pyjamas, his toothbrush and razor, the diary and address book with phone numbers, and the daily schedule for his medication. But today, my future is at stake, too; I do not want to miss this chance and I know that my father's life is not in danger. Shall I drive to him at once and postpone the interview? This is how things have always been dealt with: Father calls and helpers are on their way. We are very much back to old habits. Today, however, I do not want to play anymore.

You said you would not have minded if this had been the cause of your death.

The fall shakes my father to the core. As if dams had broken, his will to live has poured out of him like a flood. As his will to live decreases, his wish to die increases.

Father is used to having his wishes fulfilled and, if necessary, one has to lend a helping hand. He has more intensive contact with the assisted dying organisation now. The project begins to assume shape. Not before Christmas, but soon after.

The days between Christmas and New Year he spends with Angela and me in his alpine apartment in the Grisons. He is frail, but unbelievably alert. Having company and taking part in conversations makes him thrive. Starting over breakfast, he initiates philosophical discussions, listens attentively and lectures. When he cannot sleep at night, he reflects on the debates held the day before and searches for new arguments to revive the discussion the next day.

Are you asking yourself whether this is the last time that we will be in the mountains together? Or do you already know it? Have you planned your life to that extent? Have you planned your death?

*

While I am trying to collect the fragments of our joint past and combine the pieces into a big picture, Father makes plans for his future.

On my birthday in January, Father does not get in touch all day. This is unusual. I have invited a few friends and my sons to dinner. I am trying to contact my father, but he does not answer the phone. This is it, I think; he has fallen down the stairs. Perhaps his heart has given out. Or maybe he has, after all, absconded from this life, quite furtively? An acquaintance, who lives near him, makes me even more anxious: yes, she confirms, she had been shopping for him today, but found herself in front of closed doors – he had not opened. She had a key and would check at once. I would probably have to tell my guests that my father had died just now and that the dinner party was cancelled.

Fifteen minutes later, we get the all-clear. The neighbour has found him safe and sound in his four walls. Father himself calls five minutes later. He apologises for having worried us unnecessarily, explaining that he had forgotten to put back the receiver. He assumed that I was very busy throughout the day and had not wanted to call before the evening. Yet again, he had simply forgotten to put back the receiver! This is happening more and more often. Each time, I initially react with concern, then with fear. I call friends, alert neighbours, drive to his flat myself... I am starting to be frightened of the phone ringing at unusual times. My first thought is always: 'Something has happened to Father.' I am tired of these useless adrenalin rushes, these unavoidable dark thoughts! When the fear has dissolved into nothing, rage ensues.

At the beginning of February, my father has another fall. This time he breaks off his walk very shortly after leaving home, because he starts feeling dizzy. He turns around and staggers through the long underground garage looking for an entrance to the house. As he reaches the other end of the garage, he pats down the wall with his hands, but cannot find a door. In his confusion, he cannot remember where the entrance is. He is now desperate, calls for help, collapses and bangs his head hard on the concrete floor. A lot of blood, thinned by drugs for his heart condition, flows from a cut. This time the assistant gardener hears him and takes him to A&E. Later on, he is transferred to a private room for observation. He has to stay for a few days. His head injury is the least of our concerns: the recently inserted urinary catheter has caused abdominal haemorrhaging and Father has contracted a painful infection.

His mind, however, suffered the most – he is beginning to realise that he is no longer master of the situation. It could happen again, anytime and anywhere. Perhaps next time there won't be a neighbour or gardener on the spot ready to help. He is particularly devastated by the doctor's diagnosis that life without the catheter looks increasingly unlikely now. And precisely at the time when my father needs a lot of affection, most of his loved ones are far away: his partner, Bettina, is in the Emirates, Tobias Stolte on business in Singapore, Martin in Nepal. Only I am here. That is not sufficient for him.

Father is not the sort of patient who quietly tolerates an illness. He suffers noisily and expects the doctors to find a quick solution to any problem he has. If need be, the doctor is replaced by another one. The nurses get no peace, and everyone near him has to be at his beck and call. Now that the others are away and his wishes are without exception directed at me, I am getting tetchy. Instead of need, I hear only demands in his appeals – demands that brook no dissent. I am reluctant to be his dogsbody and to prioritise his requirements over mine. Just as it has always been.

You are losing control. Precisely what you never wanted to happen to you. Are the tables turning? Are the strong arguments in favour of dying unsettling you? Is it a case of 'life weighed and found wanting'?

Father resolves to take measures – not to stay alive, but to avoid an undignified death. Fall, die and not be found. Worse, still: to suffer a stroke, no longer in control of one's fate, completely helpless and at the mercy of others. His home help, a divorcee around fifty, now spends her nights in his apartment, in my mother's bedroom. I am grateful. And yet I am uneasy that a strange woman sleeps in my mother's bed.

A few days later, a private carer takes over the night shifts from the domestic help. Father does everything he can to get through the rest of his life in a dignified way. He is careful to ensure that destiny is not getting in his way.

Once more, he picks himself up. He wants to buy a reading device that enlarges book and newspaper print for him and projects it to a screen. We drive to Lucerne to consult an expert. There are only three buttons on the instrument. Too many for Father. He struggles with the machine's complex mechanical insides, but wants to take the device home to try it out – much against all advice offered. It has now been in his apartment for a week, and I don't ask how often he has used it.

Ever since he was a boy, he and technology have never seen eye to eye, and he has told me more than once – with some pride – about his approach and how successful it had always been: instead of mending his bicycle when it was broken, he preferred giving private lessons to a school friend. This way he earned enough to pay a neighbour to fix his bike and that even left him with some spare cash. Clever people are a step ahead, on the principle of 'brains not brawn'. The increasing mechanisation of everyday life showed up the loopholes in Father's concept. He had hoped to escape the digital age as its emergence coincided with his retirement. This plan, however, did not succeed.

*

During these weeks in February, I am under terrible strain. I do what I can, but what does that mean? How can I measure my competence? I could do more: I could spend every evening with him and entertain him. I could drive to him during my lunch hour. But, no, I can't. The aspiration to do more, much more, saps my strength. And it's not even my father who demands this, it is I who expects it from myself. His lifelong impatience, his subversive pressuring that has accompanied me since I was a small boy does not require words. I don't do what I could, but I can't do it anymore. This situation makes me feel selfish and heartless.

Pain, sleepless nights, indifference to what's happening in the world point my father in a certain direction. His death wish grows and he is looking for an ally. In the meantime, I understand his wish well. Angela disagrees. In her view, he suffers from age-related depression, as so many elderly do. She claims that he could be given therapy. The fact that a man so full of energy would voluntarily let go of his life is beyond comprehension for her. She rebels: she feels suffering is part of life and important during the dying process. I believe her and agree with her, but I'm on Father's side.

You say that I'm your life counsellor. I fear I do not live up to this title anymore.

Our friends are still abroad. Father hardly leaves the house, and certainly not on his own. His carer, Katharina Derungs, is now also looking after him during the day. She heats his meals and accompanies him on walks. Most importantly, she talks to him. Once or twice a day, he and I telephone each other. He has medical appointments, which are pointless and a waste of time in his opinion. When he gets up in the morning, he can't wait for it to be evening soon, but then he fears the restlessness during the night. And during the few hours of sleep he is tormented by nightmares, which play on his fear that he is not up to the challenge with which he is presented. The catheter hurts day and night. Father wants to discuss something with me.

I visit that evening in late February. Mrs Derungs has other commitments. Father comes to the door, fidgets with the catheter and pulls up his ill-fitting tracksuit bottoms. Restless nights and side-effects of medication have scarred him. His words, however, resonate with a clarity I have not heard for days. He has made a decision and worked out a time frame. He wants to take his life in just a few days. During our meal, he asks me whether I would like to be with him when he dies. The question surprises me: this role had always been Tobias Stolte's. At the time, when Father originally made the decision, he argued that this was for legal reasons. It would be possible to insinuate self-interest on the part of an heir. Assisted dying, in other words. I have to think about his question first.

Father's appearance is as pitiful as his reasoning is clear. He seems unkempt and it looks as if he could not care less. I am not used to this. He shuffles into the kitchen, his tracksuit top hanging untidily across his shoulders. Way down, at his feet, a white handkerchief is appearing out of his trouser leg. With each step more of the handkerchief emerges – I draw my father's attention to it. It's not a handkerchief, it's a nappy full of blood stains that has become loose and slipped down. Father is desperate.

On the drive home at night, the picture of overwhelming exhaustion and total surrender revived old, faded memories in me. I remember a cold January evening six years ago when I visited my terminally ill mother in hospital. I felt her rebellion, her accusations and her despair. That evening, it became clear to me that Mother had given up. She could not find the words anymore that would have allowed us to talk about it. It was as if my mother's picture had placed itself over that of my distressed father. And in their knowledge that death had knocked on the door, they resemble each other very much. The car's headlights reveal individual trees out of the darkness of the forest – for split seconds only – until the light captures a new trunk, allowing the old one to disappear into the night. The glare of an oncoming vehicle dazes me: I try to keep to my side of the road. The car whizzes past me, horn blaring. I am not concentrating.

And where is your faith? Do you not need a faith? Have you not got a faith? Do you not want a faith? Has the Church, patronising as you feel it is, taken all your faith? I would love to talk about all of this with you but do not want to get involved in an intellectual-humanist discussion about religion and enlightenment. I would like to hear straight answers, gut feelings.

Sometimes, suddenly and abruptly, unexpected thoughts turn up. I might cross the road and think to myself: everything is so normal, yet in a few days Father will be dead. How will that feel? Will he tell us when he is going to do it, will we be emotional, or will we stick to our manly stiff-upper-lip approach?

*

It is Sunday today – brilliant sunshine and spring-like temperatures. Early in the morning, Father calls Martin in Nepal. He explains to him that he wants to die now and that he cannot wait for Martin's planned visit in two months. Father says he would consider himself fortunate if he could see Martin once more, but he would understand if urgent commitments in Nepal were to prevent him from coming, or if the long journey was too arduous. My brother makes every effort to find a flight to Switzerland as fast as possible.

Angela and I fetch Father for lunch. He would like to get out. Despite a restless night and a wet bed because the catheter was not fitted properly, Father appears fresh and alert. He looks as if a great weight has shifted off his shoulders. The burden of having to come to a decision. All moaning has disappeared from our conversations; his high spirits have been transmitted to Angela and me. Instead of eating with a heavy heart, as expected, we sit at the table in a cheerful mood. Father quotes, recites and discusses. Every now and then, he comments on his impending death or issues instructions relating to it. We respond without fear and do not mind being open and frank. Now that the death has been announced and we can talk about it, the anxiety has gone. His candour and clarity help Angela see Father's decision less as a symptom of his illness and more as an act of will. 'An American Indian also decides to die', she says in the evening. It looks as if she had been able to let go. This gives me strength. We are talking about no more than days left to us.

*

Martin will be back in four days and this is an incentive for Father to put his affairs in order. There is a red folder entitled 'In the event of death' in his office in town, and he asked me to fetch it and to go through it with him in the evening. Now we sit with Tobias Stolte, bent over files and documents, checking our to-do list item by item.

Father started the red folder years ago and has always kept it up to date. A few days before my parents were going on holiday, my father used to summon me to go through the most recent version of his will. He usually began with the words: 'Should we both "get wiped out", you will find everything noted down here that needs to be done.' He chose the expression 'wiped out' deliberately – in order to remove all pathos from the perfectly real danger by talking about the possibility that our parents could lose their lives in an air crash.

In this case, the first steps would have resembled a sort of treasure hunt. Father was very careful not to discriminate against either of us, and therefore Martin and I had to take an envelope out of Father's drawer at the same time. This would have contained the instructions on how to open the safe; after opening it together, we would have taken it – with further instructions – to Tobias Stolte, who was the designated executor. Father laid great store by treating his sons fairly and equally. Money for our education, for the purchase of a house, or nursery provision for a grandchild, was always noted down meticulously so that it could be taken into account and balanced out when the estate was being distributed. When Mother died earlier than expected, he had to make major adjustments in the red folder.

'First Steps', 'Death Notice', 'Circulation', 'Last Will', even the biography that will be read out at the funeral service and distributed with the letters announcing the death have all been meticulously prepared. We go through every point, check its validity and discuss any ambiguities. Should the service be held for close family only, or does the announcement have to give information on time and venue? In that case, this would turn into a major event – the price for a life lived in the public eye.

Father is getting tired. He is not interested in details and he does not care who needs power of attorney for what reason after his death. He does care, however, and up to the last hour, that everything runs fairly and correctly. The conversation with him does me good. I am involved, I do not have to put up with anything passively and nothing is being decided above my head. My advice is sought and I may have a say. I am less frightened of all the administrative tasks Father's death will bring in its wake. I would love to tell him that. I would also like to ask him whether he now feels relieved and if he is afraid. This, however, is not something one talks about: typical for our family. We function wonderfully well in times of crisis, but not when it comes to emotions – that is our weak point. I think that the feelings will perhaps follow later on.

Tobias Stolte takes his leave. In a few minutes, Bettina will visit. My father and I are alone for a short time. He confides in me that Katharina Derungs, his carer, knows of his plan. And that he is concerned about Bettina. Bettina, having found him determined and ready to die on her return from her holidays, now oscillates between understanding and grief. Father seems to be looking for a way to obtain her consent, too.

You can still turn back or pause. Even when Martin returns from Nepal to say goodbye to you, you should not feel under an obligation to act. You can continue to live if you want to.

Bettina appears tense. As soon as she has taken off her coat to sit with us, Father barges in with a request: could she send me the address list of the people to be notified of his death, please? She had looked after the file over the years and kept it up-to-date. I should now print it out in a large font and pass it on to him so that he could correct it. Since it was last revised four years ago, many contacts had

74

themselves died. Bettina's lips have narrowed. She wants nothing to do with this. She has come in order to talk about matters of principle, not trivial stuff. 'What can I do for you to regain your enjoyment of life?' she asks abruptly. My father is surprised, talks about the pains his catheter causes, the bedwetting, the loss of dignity. He seems uncertain, however. He has not found any convincing arguments to win his partner over. I am slightly annoyed, as Bettina has made him brood again. I don't know what drives her: selfishness or the belief that Father is not yet ready to die? Her question is, after all, a fair one. I, too, am now rattled. Is my support correct, or should I wake the fighter in him? Does Bettina expect my help?

I am sitting between Father and Bettina. They conduct a discussion in a self-conscious way, just as if I were preventing them from talking to each as they normally do. 'I think this is something you should talk about on your own', I say and ask myself at the same time why this should be so. I have already reached the door, however, and nobody has stopped me.

*

My suspicions were correct. Bettina blames herself that she cannot pass on sufficient love of life to my father. She also believes that he would not have decided to die if she had been at his side in the last few days. And she finds fault with the way Father, Tobias Stolte and I addressed the matter, namely in a far too clinical, unemotional way. My father is no longer so sure about his decision: he wants me to visit him.

Katharina Derungs, elegant, discreet and used to working in sophisticated circles, opens the door. Despite her reserve, she radiates warmth, which is obviously good for Father. She reports that she has taken a walk with him in the morning. 'We have laughed a lot', she says in her soft voice. This is the best thing I heard that day.

Father and I have lunch together. Katharina Derungs serves the food, already familiar with Father's impatience when it comes to the smooth progress of mealtimes. Matters become complex: Bettina is sad because she cannot motivate Father to continue to live, and Father is sad because he cannot dissuade Bettina from her belief that she is responsible for him wanting to die. Father therefore hesitates – not because he has regained any *joie de vivre*, but because he is tormented by feelings of duty and responsibility. When he dies, he wants to be sure that the lives of his loved ones are in order and safe. Bettina's despair does not fit well into this scenario. Whoever proceeds on the assumption that they can control, and have power over, the welfare of others clearly acts presumptuously. I argue forcefully. Neither he nor Bettina could be held responsible for the other's good fortune.

You were silent and you nodded.

I cannot let go of the matter that afternoon. Throughout his life, Father has taken responsibility. This is what he enjoys and this is how he wields influence. He supports other people, even when he cannot possibly benefit. The only condition is that the goals do not run counter to his ideals. But selfless he is not. He is determined, he takes what he wants and he gets it, too. Now he wants to take his own life. Enough is enough.

*

Our occasional conversations have turned into a rolling dialogue. Father keeps calling me, over and over, to ensure

I am up to date. He gives me the latest 'bulletin', so to speak, and asks me for my opinion. His insecurity adds even more weight to my role as his counsellor. But I am not playing a part on stage, I am talking about a life. And to put it bluntly, a human life – perhaps in its last act.

It seems as if Father is happy to accept any advice, as long as it exempts him from having to take decisions himself. He trusts my advice and objections unreservedly, but also uses them not to have to carry all the responsibility himself. I want to be an advisor, but not an influence. Will my support, based on my own experiences and by what I myself have suffered in the past, meet his needs? Will I be able to stand by my guidance even after his death?

My father tells me that Bettina had received backing from an unexpected source. Ralph Troxler, Father's longstanding confidant at the assisted dying organisation, had reassured him that he could make use of the group's services and that he was, indeed, free to determine the date and time himself. In the end, though, Troxler asked himself if Father, with all his vitality and creativity, had actually reached this point. My father will meet him for lunch tomorrow – two men who had, up to now, always agreed about the matter of dying, perhaps with different views after all? The man in favour of dying makes the case for life? This does not fit into my picture of an assisted dying organisation, and I wonder whether he has a selfish intention: it would not look good if it became known that his organisation helped my father, a model of vitality in old age, to die. Precisely at the time when assisted dying is being increasingly talked about, headlines of this type would not be welcome. No doubt Father pays for the image he presents in public: strong, steely, perceptive and eloquent. He shows his weak, vulnerable side and his great fear of suddenly losing self-determination to only few people. I am one of them. I am honoured, but it does not make things easier.

This is not how you had imagined it to be. You wanted to depart without a big fuss. But believe me, you are doing well. I am proud of you. You have summoned up the courage to confront your loved ones with your intentions and you are prepared to put up with opposition. This is how you have lived and you ought to be able to die the same way.

*

I withdraw my allegations against Ralph Troxler. Father reports that Troxler had not in the least tried to talk him out of his intentions. He had wanted to see him and tell him how much he regretted that they had not met before. He felt sure that they could have given each other a lot. Ralph Troxler is a theologian and he loves thinking about what this world is all about.

I shall pick up Martin from the airport in a few hours. He will stay with Angela and me and I am looking forward to having him near me. He is my older brother and even if the difference in age has lost its importance over the decades, I sense that I have been waiting for the moment when I could pass on the burden of responsibility to my older sibling. This is how we dealt with such matters when we were children, and this is how it should be done now. There are questions that I have to answer myself: how and when do I inform my sons Mathias and Fabian? How do I tell Evelyne, their mother, who was my father's daughter-in-law for thirty years? I am trying to convince Father that it is important for them that he talks to them personally, and that I would under no circumstances conceal the truth. My father has chosen next Thursday as the date for his death.

*

The question whether I will be present at his death has not been answered. 'With his loved ones by his side', as death announcements normally say. I always imagine this to be an enriching and peaceful experience. Is this also true for those who opt for assisted dying?

Death has been kept away from me for a long time. Nobody ever talked to me about the process of dying, neither in my childhood nor in my youth. And, as far as the dying or the deceased went, I was definitely not expected to give them another thought. As I grew older, this irritated me. Although I had known all my grandparents, I did not attend any of their funerals. When the last one took place, I was twenty-two years old and lived abroad, but not far from home – my mother told me that it was not necessary for me to come home especially. I accepted this without complaint and did not wish to oppose my mother's wishes. For me, it seemed normal to stay clear of death whenever possible. Death is horrible, life is good – that was roughly the message I had taken from my youth into adulthood. I was fifty when I first saw a dead human being. That was my mother.

I would have liked to talk with her about her approaching death. It would have been good for all of us. But we waited until Mother could not talk and think anymore. I am, to this day, still bothered by this. The dying suppress the truth because they want to spare their loved ones. And the living attempt, against their better judgement, to encourage the dying to hold out with the remark 'I am sure it will be ok.' For life's sake, lies are told to the last breath.

*

The time with Father melts away – it feels like water running through my fingers. It takes a lot of strength not to focus on his dying but on my life. The day of today tears shreds from the energy layer that has surrounded me like a protective corset. At work, everything goes wrong. And at the airport I have to wait two full hours for my friends Anja and Malte, who arrive late from Hamburg – we had planned to have a week's holiday in the mountains together. They will have to spend the days in Father's apartment without me. Even if we were together, my father would come between us. I tell them that Father is very ill and that I cannot leave him alone. The car journey to the Prättigau is long and congested, and the return trip to Zurich – after midnight – is barely tolerable. In the meantime, I function with precision and without emotion, just as I did in Darien: taking one moment at a time, never losing concentration, making no mistakes and not allowing feelings to creep in. I am very good at that, but I exploit body and soul, burning the candle at both ends. It is only a matter of time before my body will revolt.

Today is Saturday, and the three of us – Martin, Angela (who is only at home at weekends because of her current work schedule) and I – talk continually about what is, what will be and what was at some time in the past. We now have to string together the lives of a father and his two sons like the links of a chain. While we talk, we change the formation of our little group – always close to total exhaustion.

You are, yet again, incredibly demanding, dear Father. How shall we handle you during these last days? What is good for you and what is good for us?

Martin fears that the final days will neither work out according to his wishes nor according to his needs. Since he was young, too much has built up between him and Father for so many years – issues have become stuck and hardened, and now there is no chance of thrashing them out. The remaining days will not allow discussions to resolve anything. Angela's point of view helps him, helps us. She is sufficiently distanced to draw our attention to the positions that we took as children and which we have not left since then. She helps us look at matters from another angle.

I am still struggling with the question as to whether I want to be with my father when he dies. Suddenly, I feel compelled to stay with him to the end of the path. This would, however, be terrifying and inconceivable for my brother Martin. How could he share an act of such intimacy with other people, strangers even, with Tobias Stolte, Ralph Troxler, perhaps with Bettina or Katharina Derungs, who are all unfamiliar to him? We approach the decision from different angles, but neither of us is here yet.

*

Mathias calls early in the morning and wants to know what on earth is going on here. Why is his Uncle Martin coming to Zurich right now and why is his family not coming with him? If it has anything to do with his grandfather, what has happened? I don't want to keep them in the dark and repeat Father's mistakes, when he excluded us from his sister's death. I call my father and tell him that I will, this very day, inform Evelyne, Mathias and Fabian. Father agrees. He wants to talk to Evelyne himself. Until lately he was unwilling to disclose his intention to anyone. Tobias Stolte was to inform us all, after his death, that he had died of a heart attack. Now he has come to the view that at least his family has the right to learn the truth.

Shortly after noon, I meet Evelyne, Mathias and Fabian. I describe Father's state of mind, his physical condition, tell them about how he came to feel that he had had enough of life and how his decision to take his own life slowly matured. This does not come as a great surprise for Evelyne; she has known Father's attitude for a long time. Mathias feels that such matters should be left to each individual, but he says that he wants to visit his grandfather once more. Fabian remains silent. They accept Father's decision to depart this life with the support of an assisted dying organisation. What they find more difficult to accept is that the circumstances must be kept secret. They do not want to be forced to lie to their friends – and this is just how I feel. I sense a great burden falling from me because I do not have to conceal anything from them, at least. And if I think about it more precisely, I do not want to withhold the truth from my friends and acquaintances, either – whether Father likes it or not.

At home, during the late afternoon, I have another discussion with Martin. We support each other, revive old memories from our youth, some filed away casually, some carefully. How was it exactly? What was cause and what was effect in the events of the late 1960s? How did we react to our parents' decisions? How did they deal with our protests? Mother once said that they had believed it necessary to nip things in the bud and that they had never reckoned social order would be turned upside down to such an extent. What has shaped Martin and me? What was Father's part in this and how did Mother influence us?

We also talk about what is important for us in these days before Father's death. The central question remains: whether we shall be with him when he dies. If he wants me to be near him, I shall accompany him all the way to the end. I do not want to cop out. I am sure that afterwards I shall be glad that there are no questions unanswered about Father's final hours. Martin is an attentive listener. He is struck by my view that it would be cowardly to dodge our father's wish to have us there. Neither of us can invoke ethical reasons: we acknowledge his right to come to a free decision. Can Martin bear these last minutes with Father, though? He fears that Father might, after all, be uncharacteristically emotional at the end. Perhaps he would panic after having drunk the deadly potion? And he could hardly tolerate the presence of strange people who would share this intimate moment with him. But he does not want to be accused of cowardice. Martin and I agree to accompany Father together, or not at all. The situation calls for a unified stance.

In the evening, we conduct the by now obligatory phone conversation with our father: we simply inform each other what the latest state of affairs is. Father has arranged an appointment for us with Ralph Troxler, the representative of the assisted dying organisation. This is the result of Martin's insistence to learn more about the process and ramifications of assisted dying. Father now also knows who will accompany him during his final hours. He and Bettina have talked about it again and agreed that she would be with him. He said he would welcome it, if he could take leave of us over a meal the night before. But should we come to the conclusion that we wanted to accompany him to the very end, after all, he would say goodbye to Bettina the evening before.

Even during the final hours, things that had always been kept separate may not now grow together. Ultimately, this matches reality, of course. Father has always lived in different, distinct worlds, which he rarely brought together. I think Bettina feels, just like Martin, that she does not want to give free rein to her feelings in front of people with whom she is not familiar – and that includes us. Martin is relieved that he does not have to accompany Father into death in the presence of strangers. To be sure, Father lets us choose, but I respect his wish, of course. At least I have the certainty that he will not be carelessly removed from life, so to speak: Bettina will definitely make sure of that. I shall have to live with the fact that my father's final hours will remain concealed from me – it is currently not very clear to me what has actually been arranged and agreed.

*

Angela is frightened of today, Sunday. Father would like to have lunch with Martin and me in the Restaurant Sternen. It will be the usual table – in this restaurant, too; my father has secured 'his' corner table for himself for decades. The thought of sitting at the 'farewell table' makes her feel sick. Angela calls it that because we sat at this very table with Martin and Tim before they left for Nepal. This will be the last time that she sees Father and will talk to him. She is afraid to be left alone with her feelings in our world of men.

Angela and my father have known each other for a few years. She had missed her own father when she was a child and, in mine, she had met a man who approached her in an unexpectedly relaxed and fatherly way. He was someone who listened to her, who engaged with her and who challenged her in her intellectual world. Angela wishes that he would want to continue to live.

She would love nothing better than to stay at home. She fears that the bright, clear memory of last Sunday's meal together could become blurred and gloomy. I ask her to join us so that I don't have to bear the tensions between my brother and father alone. Angela accompanies us. To my surprise the meal proceeds in harmony, without hidden messages and silent reproaches. Martin and Father have come out of their trenches.

We drive to Father's apartment today as well. In my head, I still see the sad farewell pictures between my father and brother of more than six months ago – they are images full of helplessness and emotional emptiness. Angela will do this better. She wants to be alone when the two say goodbye. Martin and I wait in the garage, while Angela takes Father's arm and accompanies him upstairs to the flat. It must have been a beautiful, warm leave-taking between the two of them, and of course a painful one as well. Angela returns with tears in her eyes. There is nothing to be said; we drive home in silence.

*

I am celebrating my fifteenth anniversary at work. To mark the occasion, my company offers to give me half of a monthly salary or an additional two weeks' holiday. Only a few days ago, I would have chosen the money, but right now time is important for me; I need the additional days to recover from the current stress.

A client cancels his contract, Mathias telephones to say that he passed his university exams, Fabian gives me an update on his job search and Angela sends a text message about the care of a particularly difficult patient. What I would normally have taken an active interest in, I am simply letting roll off my shoulders. I cannot deal with more; each bit of news is one too many. I make a note indicating 'absence' in the diary, starting with the day of Father's death and ending with the date of the planned memorial service. Looks like holidays.

Just this minute, Father has telephoned to announce a 'programme change'. He has obviously planned something again without giving those affected enough time to consider it. Bettina has decided overnight that she does not wish to be present when Father is dying, unless he gives her no other option: she would not be able to cope. That, however, Father does not want to do, so we, his sons, are again his first choice. Father calls to ask if we are ready. I am ready, more than ever, but I doubt that Martin shares my view. Yesterday, he appeared to be relieved about Father's wish to have Bettina with him at his death. The decision is now back with him – and with me; we had, after all, agreed to take the same position. On this, I am not so certain anymore. What's so important about being unified on this? For me, what I can best live with afterwards has become more important. I hope this will be clear when Martin and I meet Ralph Troxler from the assisted dying organisation.

At four o'clock in the afternoon, Martin and I have an appointment with Ralph Troxler in a restaurant. My brother has called the meeting because he wants to know if we, as direct heirs, can be prosecuted for being Father's companions at his death. Troxler says 'no'. He confirms that he is aware of these fears but assures us that the Swiss Criminal Code is unambiguous on this point. If anyone were culpable, it would be him. He will, after all, bring the lethal substance and it will be him who hands Father the potion to drink. He argues in a detached and composed way. He knows how important it is to dispel the doubts some relatives have. He tells us that he has become a good friend of Father's over the last few years, that they have talked regularly and that they are very much kindred spirits. It is of course possible that their shared humanistic world view and their understanding with regard to decisions on death and dying link the two men. But friendship?

Ralph Troxler will be the 'angel of death' who enables Father's final journey – he considers it a favour for a friend. He describes the procedure and what we should expect if we are present. The detailed explanations suddenly allow us to form an opinion and to assess the situation; my worries subside. Troxler again quotes the relevant sections of the law and repeats convincingly that we do not have to be afraid of legal consequences. Martin relaxes, partly because it becomes clear that, apart from us, only Troxler would be there. Neither Tobias Stolte, who had for years been designated to do my father this favour, nor Bettina, or an unknown witness, would be present. Martin can live with this. This is the moment when it becomes obvious that we shall accompany Father together when he dies. Troxler does not conceal either that the police and the public prosecutor will turn up at the house shortly after Father's death, because it will be categorised as an 'extraordinary death'. In these cases, the police have to be notified immediately.

We ask Ralph Troxler if he, as a vicar, would like to conduct the funeral. Troxler has been a parish priest, but he hesitates. He points out that people could put two and two together if he, a representative of the assisted dying organisation, officiated. This is immaterial, because it was Father's wish to have only close family at the ceremony and everyone present will, in any case, be aware of how he wanted to die. I prefer to have a person take the funeral who has engaged in long philosophical discussions with him and who knows his rejection of clerical pretentions, rather than a vicar who has never met him in all his life. Troxler agrees.

On the way home I feel relieved, because I now *know* what to expect at Father's death. At the same time, I am anxious, since every clarification of detail leads us ever more inescapably to the action that is planned: the designation of location and time, the process, the identification of the people who will be there. Planning is meticulous – the same way it would be for an execution. Accidents are precluded. The practicalities do not seem to equate with this decisive moment in a man's life. On the other hand, are agonising pain, breathlessness and the hectic atmosphere of an intensive care unit any better?

*

Planning gathers its own momentum and starts to take over. Everything that is in its way is being crushed. Nothing can thrive in this situation except for new plans, some looking beyond Father's death: How on earth can his death be kept secret for about six days? Who may be let in on it and who may not? We want to be sure that the funeral is not going to be a grand affair. As if it were a game of strategy, I think about where traps or obstacles could endanger the plan; I am trying to see through other players' moves. This matches my state of mind precisely: the planned arrangements simply have to work, there must be no mistakes, everything has to be under control. I worry about this more than Martin and feel on my own.

Normally, I would have asked you for advice. You would certainly have commended your military tactics to me. Plan for the long term, prepare well. But always build a fallback position and new trenches into which you can withdraw when the enemy has overrun the first line.

I now take Father's evening call so much for granted and it is such a familiar ritual that I cannot imagine that there will be an end to it. Today, he says: 'The firing squad comes at ten o'clock.' Humour is good, but it disguises the risk that an act may be robbed of the dignity it deserves.

At night I am awake for a long time. My head feels like a one-armed bandit in an amusement arcade. You pull the lever and colourful icons rush past me. You push a button and stop the train of thoughts. Sometimes nothing fits together, but sometimes it still does. For example: the 'ius primae noctis', an old law under which feudal lords and slave owners had the right to have sex with a subordinate woman on the first night of her marriage – before her husband. Is there a 'ius ultimae diei', a right of the last day? Who is entitled to spend the final hours with someone who dies? Who may claim this right, who will enforce it, who will dodge the responsibility? Is there a duty as well as a right? Or is everything just pure coincidence, after all? But someone has already pulled the lever again and the pictures are racing on . . .

*

I visit Father over midday. Katharina Derungs has prepared a meal for us. We toast each other with a glass of good wine just as we have always done when we had one of our traditional lunch meetings in town. We do not drink to a long life, to a specific success or to the years spent together. We simply nod to each other. We both know that this is our last meal together. Tomorrow, the day before Father's death, Martin will have lunch with him. In the evening, Bettina will sit at the table with him for the last time.

You are in control again: you have arranged everything in your power and are in a mood for joking. Your grandsons are visiting in the afternoon, and in the early evening Evelyne will come to say goodbye. This is exactly as you want it, you say. Are you pulling the wool over my eyes, are you fooling the world in order to keep up appearances, or are you serious this time?

On my way back to work, I am beginning to feel sad. It is a big, soothing sadness, supported by a deep, inner peace. I am grateful for the minutes alone in the car – I think back to the meals we had together. During Father's best times they were rare occurrences, because his diary did not permit spontaneous entries. My hippy phase and his world of management did not really mix well. Later on, when I had a proper career myself and he had retired, it became easier. Sometimes, he sought a confidential chat to discuss a family matter, at other times, I sought his advice about a professional or tactical issue. After Mother's death, our luncheon rituals became more regular. Father frequented a couple of restaurants where he always booked 'his' table; for example, in the 'Hongkong', in the 'Da Angelo', or in the sophisticated 'Eden', which was only chosen for special occasions. One of the rituals consisted in ordering a 'Dreierli',[6] knowing full well that it would not be enough. Father would slightly tilt his head as he savoured the first sip and say: 'Good, but I doubt that it will be enough.' Sometimes I was embarrassed when he chased the waiters around impatiently, because he wanted the courses to be served without any pauses, or when he insisted on getting a carafe of lukewarm tap water. Another ritual was his demand for a little sweet titbit, or a piece of chocolate with his coffee. He got what he wanted. I shall miss these meals and the conversations, of course. Today, however, my sorrow is not painful – it is characterised by the certainty that I shall continue to carry my father inside me.

---

[6] Open wine served in a three-decilitre carafe.

Back in my office, I tell a colleague why I want to take a few days of vacation. I can trust her, and our friendship means too much for me to lie to her through my teeth. We are very close. In her office, I can calm down and regain my strength again, as if we were in an oasis. The corridors outside and the meeting rooms are like a desert where storms prevent us seeing into the future and where shifting quick-sand threatens to carry me away.

An hour later, I meet up with Mathias in a pub around the corner. He has come from meeting his grandfather; it had been a good farewell, and this meant a lot to him. He said that his grandfather had stood by him during important phases of his life. For this, he had wanted to thank him again.

More than once, Father said that Martin and I were better fathers. He was sorry that he had not been able to make more time for us. He had given his career priority. It had, for example, been impossible to allow a business meeting to fall through in order to participate at a son's birthday party. When he became a grandfather, he made up for it, doing things for which he had not had time when Martin and I were growing up. When Mathias had serious difficulties at school, his grandfather crammed Latin into him. This was not done in line with modern didactic methods: conjugations and declensions were practised mercilessly. Mathias had himself chosen his grandfather to be his tutor: he knew that he would learn with him. Next term, Latin was already no longer an issue. Nobody was as keen as my father that his three grandsons' handshakes were firm and that they made eye contact when they greeted someone. If they forgot, he corrected them at once. On one occasion, the seventy-year-old visited the Natural History Museum in Basel with the six- and the eight-year-old. He had prepared himself meticulously and put together an educational programme for the day. Exhausted from the teaching, he fell asleep on the train journey home. The grandsons had to wake him up at the railway station in Zurich.

In the evening, I say goodbye to Anja and Malte at the airport. I had talked to Anja almost every day during her stay in the Grisons. Her uplifting sense of humour and her evident joy about the beautiful days they spent in the mountains exhilarated me for some precious moments each time we spoke. Shortly before going through passport control, she hands me a thank-you letter for my father. I cannot tell her that he will die the day after tomorrow. But I shall make sure that he reads the letter.

On the way home on the motorway, weariness hangs on me like lead. How fast the white dividing lines speed by. My eyes are fixed on the red rear lights of the car in front of me, a round one on the left and on the right, with an oblong one above the rear window. I am trying to keep the distance to them always the same and concentrate to avoid crossing the white lines under my wheels. I cannot focus anymore. I turn the car radio on and hear that a 'Doors-Special' is playing. The Doors are tormenting me even more: I can literally, as it were, smell my dreary teenage years through them. The presenter announces the song 'Five to One', and Jim Morrison's strident voice forces its way through the loudspeaker grille.

Do you hear, Father? Jim Morrison is right, there are no two ways about it: 'No one here gets out alive.'

Minutes later, I am in the rest area under the trees whose leafless branches hang over the windscreen like skeletons: I should have switched off the radio when they put on 'The

End'. Instead, I turned up the volume and got off the motorway. 'The End' – that is another story. An oppressive song that stirs dark memories of injury and self-harm; Jim Morrison's text, a provocation for fathers and mothers, my companion in rebellion and fury.

Have we left all this behind us, Father?

When we talk late in the evening, his account of the afternoon's meetings is concise and terse. He had, admittedly, mastered the farewells brilliantly, but also reluctantly, first from my sons and then from Evelyne. He reports that there were tears. This is something he still cannot deal with, even now. He grumbles jokingly, not without expressing his displeasure: 'Next time I wish to die, I shall first enter a monastery so that I can pull this off on my own.' I tell him that this is a good idea; this way he could compare later on which solution was better and more sustainable in the long term. In fact, I don't feel like cracking jokes anymore. The day has been intense with a rich programme: the constant changes of scene and mood have taken their toll. My nerves are taut and even Martin's presence is too much for me tonight.

*

Today I am free from Father. We do not have a meal together and I do not expect changes to the programme anymore. It is the turn of others: Martin will have lunch with him and Bettina will visit him in the evening.

I am simply doing my job today and am surprised that this works so well. How can I put sales records together, get angry about a colleague's mistake and find a teammate's behaviour courageous? How can I eat barley soup in the staff dining room and be annoyed that the outside of the salad dressing bottle is greasy?

The canteen is crammed full of people and while I sit there, I ask myself: how would these people react if I got up and said: 'My father will die tomorrow.'

When it's time to go home, my colleagues wish me a nice holiday. After work, I go to the indoor swimming pool. Father has given me a year's subscription for my birthday. It seems fitting that I use it tonight. Concentrating on my movements is good for me: I enjoy the feeling of the water lifting up my body, making it buoyant, and I hear how the air I breathe out under water releases regular bubbles. I swim backstroke for a few lanes, focusing on the black line in the ceiling and count my strokes: eleven, twelve, thirteen. Then I touch the side of the pool with my hand, turn around and start afresh: one, two, three . . . No other thought can squeeze itself between the numbers.

Everything is prepared. I am not afraid. You do not have to worry about me. What you wanted to give me, you have already given, and it will remain with me: your death will not change this.

Tonight, my father and Bettina will say goodbye to each other. He will ensure that the food is excellent and the wine exquisite. Conversation will be sophisticated, laced with a few bons mots. He will be strong, and Bettina as strong as possible – just like always, really.

What will Father think of when he goes to bed tonight? Will he think: is this my last night? Will he recall scenes from his life? Will he immerse himself in key experiences, pull out the most beautiful moments and weep quietly to himself? Will he allow thoughts to stir that have been pushed aside till now because he always felt uneasy about them? Will he have nagging doubts? Or will he just fall asleep tired from the wine and the sleeping pills? Will he wake up and go to the bathroom like every night, or will everything be different?

Martin has prepared dinner for us. He is busy with pots and pans, dwelling on his thoughts – what happened once and what will be tomorrow. Everything he does is normal; he moves as if nothing were unusual. He scrapes the salad bowl with his spoon as he always does, he stacks the dishwasher in the way that is so familiar to me, and he has, of course, practised lighting his cigarette a thousand times – with a mere click. Here and now everything is much the same as ever, and tomorrow the extraordinary will happen. Martin says: 'Well, we shall survive even this.' Yes, we shall, indeed.

*

Day of the execution. I get up shortly before seven o'clock. It is getting light already: the pale hazy blue sky will slowly be immersed into the cool yellow of the morning sunlight. There is no doubt: today is a brilliant spring day. 'What a good day to die!'[7] Yesterday, I was thinking what I would wear, what befitted the occasion, and have settled on jeans, turtleneck pullover and a jacket. Father impressed on us yesterday that we had to arrive on time, at half past nine. I dress – calmly and focused – simply glad that it is going to be a bright day. Shortly before eight o'clock, I wake Martin. We leave the apartment in time to make sure that we are punctual. We stop over at Moosweiher, a little lake in the forest only five minutes from Father's home. We are a bit early and that gives Martin another opportunity to smoke a cigarette. After that, we drive to Father's apartment.

As we get out of the car, I see Father at once: he stands on the balcony, smiling, holding onto Katharina Derungs' arm and enjoying the sun. The two of them appear like a royal couple showing themselves on a special occasion, a birthday, a coronation or an official reception to accept the people's homage. They seem so comfortable and familiar with each other. In truth, I feel that Katharina Derungs would have been a perfect partner for my father. Father is

---

[7] Hokahey! or 'Today is a good day to die' is a phrase historically associated with certain Native American cultures.

clean shaven and has dressed in a fawn suit with a matching tie. After a short welcome, he leads us to the suite of chairs in the living room where he wants to die. Katharina Derungs pointed out to him a week ago that dying in the first-floor bedroom might be complicated. The coffin could not be easily transported down the narrow, circular staircase. The funeral directors would first have to transport Father's lifeless body downstairs to place him into the coffin. In any case, we all think that the living room is a more beautiful place to die. We can all sit together here and make him comfortable on the sofa when the time comes.

Before we sit down, Father hands me his wallet and his watch. He would not be needing either anymore. This is a very personal gesture and comes across as final. These two possessions, which my father hardly ever laid down, were simply part of him and accompanied him everywhere – he hands them over in the way one hands over one's belongings and weapon at the end of a tour of military service. He also pressed an envelope with eight-thousand francs into my hand so that any expenses arising from his death can be covered at once. He would not wish us to have to rely on our own resources. I put the items with appropriate care and respect into the depths of the bag I had brought with me.

Father firmly motions everyone to their allocated place in the group of chairs. He does it in his relaxed and calm way, very attentive, perhaps a bit impatient. On the little side table there is a bottle of 1967 Château d'Yquem. A third has been drunk. He tells us that he had opened it yesterday, when Bettina was visiting to say goodbye. They had eaten something delicious, drunk this wine and talked. Yes, Bettina had been sad.

Martin and I do not want to drink anything yet; we would like to wait for Ralph Troxler. Then we can clink glasses – toast life, death? Perhaps simply the time we were allowed to spend together. Katharina Derungs removes the wine, puts it into a cool place and brings some water. Father waits for ten o'clock. He does not want to have a tediously slow leave-taking, no sentimentalities. It should just happen now. The whole living room is flooded with sunlight. It seems as if there were not a single dark corner in this apartment. I wonder what the experience this morning would be like if it were grey and rainy outside. Luckily, this is not the case.

I join Katharina Derungs in the kitchen, where she remains, unobtrusively, but always at the ready in case she can help. I would like to know how Father's night had been. She smiles. She thinks that he slept well; she had heard little from him and the bladder catheter had not bothered him. She only wonders how this small, 3dl red wine bottle has turned up in the kitchen; last night, when Father had already gone to bed and she had switched the lights off, it was not there. The old gentleman had obviously indulged in a little glass when he could no longer sleep early in the morning.

Well done. You have treated yourself to something good. I hope that there was no shortage of wine and that the memories that passed through your mind were pleasant. Where were you? At home in your nursery, with your sisters, at school with your friend Breitenstein, or were you doing active military service with your comrades, defending Switzerland? Were Martin and I there, too? Was Mother there?

Shortly after ten, Ralph Troxler arrives, a battered old briefcase in his hand, which he puts inconspicuously next to the little coffee table. He sits down next to my father on the wide sofa – in accordance with Father's instructions. Martin and I sit on the second, slightly smaller, sofa. Frau Derungs brings the wine and passes a few nibbles around. Father asks if he is also allowed to eat something and Troxler agrees that this would be fine, as long as it is not too rich.

This was just like the scene at Father's last birthday: sitting in this apartment, with savoury snacks, wine and clever speeches. Today, Father takes the seat that was allocated to the friend he had rejected. He chose this group of chairs for dying because the light beige sofa with the delicate tartan pattern is long enough to lie down on. Otherwise, there are only big armchairs in this room.

We clink glasses, today also without proposing a grand toast. Someone puts some words together about our shared history – I have forgotten who it was. I see my father and Troxler with glasses in their hands and feel Martin next to me. While I raise my glass to my mouth, I am pondering where Father, Martin and I were when the grapes were harvested in that autumn. There will never again be a reunion in this configuration. We are a four-man community of fate. 'Fate' sounds as if only coincidence had brought us together here today. But our getting together is the result of active efforts, which means that there has to be a 'perpetrator' and if there is a perpetrator there are victims, as well. Is Father a perpetrator or victim or both? On which side are Martin and I?

Ralph Troxler is keen to keep a serious conversation going and makes Father aware that he means a lot to him. For me, this feels like an admirable combination of genuine affection and professional duty. Troxler is completely focused on Father, which means that Martin and I turn from involved actors to extras.

Memories of conversations we had during meals when I was a young teenager are inadvertently and without prompting conjured up: in those days, my parents often quarrelled with Martin when the family sat at the table; first Mother about the length of his hair and the shape of his trousers when 'The Twist' was in fashion, and later on, more fiercely, Father about imperialism, exploitation, and law and order. I was too small, and was never asked for my opinion – I had to stay outside, like the dog outside the butcher's. Today my brother and I are, of course, on the same side; the two men discuss belief, the views of Dietrich Bonhoeffer and Karl Barth, with Father repeatedly asking what the time is. He tries to hurry up the final act by saying: 'Well, my dear chap, you will now no doubt explain to me the procedure in detail.' But Troxler does not want to be rushed. I hear more snippets of conversation and know that Troxler pulls a little bottle out of his briefcase, pouring its contents into a glass of water. Father wants to know if this is the cup of hemlock. Troxler says that it is not. It is merely medication to stop him being sick, just in case. Father looks around, confirming once more that he has had a good life and that he lacked nothing. He includes us, his sons, in this acknowledgement of being fortunate. That made us feel good.

After another twenty minutes crammed full of clever sentences and without any pause or rest, Ralph Troxler takes a second little brown glass bottle from his briefcase. He shakes the viscous sodium pentobarbital vigorously and asks Father whether he had really thought about this thoroughly, saying that it would be no problem to stop now. Father is irritated, as if he thought: 'But we have been there already.' His intention is unwavering. Troxler pours the contents of the flask into a glass and explains what will happen now. Father could remain sitting until he had emptied the glass – it might perhaps take between three and ten minutes; this varied greatly between individuals. He would then simply fall asleep. The physical capacities would go and, finally, his breathing. By then, he would no longer feel anything. He hands my father the glass.

'Hans, this tastes very bitter.'

'Not to worry; this is not the bitterest thing I have had to swallow in my life.'

Father poured the medication down his throat in one go. Troxler asks me to add some water to the glass so that Father can rinse down the drug. After that, my father leans back and begins to talk again – about life, and that he was glad to be able to abdicate, reminding everyone that so many of his friends had already gone. Father yawns heartily, really loudly, as if he was looking forward to the forthcoming sleep. His whole body relaxes.

'Yes, my three best friends have all taken their own lives', he says, and his eyelids become heavy.

He does not look over to us again. His head bends down again. But he talks.

'The first threw himself under a train, the second shot himself with his gun, and the third jumped from the Basler Wettsteinbrid…'

And then, my father falls asleep. Soundly, with finality. The three of us put him to bed on the sofa. Troxler goes away, to the back part of the room, Martin sits at the head of the bed and I sit next to Father's knees and hold his hands, which are folded over his stomach. They are soft and warm. Father's chest rises and sinks gently and regularly, but slightly less with every breath. I cannot tell any more whether he is still breathing, but I can see the regular pulse in his jugular. It is a peaceful moment. The sun gives everything a friendly light; there is not a hint of darkness, nor any feeling of oppression to burden my soul. The pulse becomes increasingly weak until this last sign of life stops, too. I continue to look at Father and to stroke his hands. My hands run over his arm and stay on his chest. Now he rests, the great man, even in death quite the gentleman. He who could enthuse and sweep so many along with great words and strong deeds is silent. My father is dead.

Stop the time, preserve the moment as it is – I wish I could do it. Twenty minutes after Father fell asleep, Ralph Troxler approaches the death bed. He checks Father's silenced heartbeat and pupillary reflexes. He confirms that he is sure Father is dead. He informs us that he will now have to notify the police and that it will take perhaps thirty minutes or an hour before they arrive. He tells us to leave the glass my father drank as evidence, in case the police want to examine it. The medical officer and the public prosecutor would presumably come, too. It could be unpleasant.

I have no idea what Troxler means by that and I am not yet prepared to leave this silence and return to normal daily life. I go into the kitchen and tell Katharina Derungs that Father has died. She gets up from the table and approaches the death bed, lost in her own thoughts. Delicately, she fastens the three buttons on Father's jacket and carefully tugs at his sleeve until she considers it perfectly arranged. He would have loved her for this! She leans over Father gently, puts her hand on his hand and says goodbye to him – the man she had been so close to in the last few days. There is a contented smile on her face, as if she wanted to show that everything turned out just as my father had wanted. 'He looks so peaceful', she says. There is nothing disconcerting in this. Katharina Derungs's caring gestures, which had not left any trace on Father's life until a few days ago, are full of respect, intimate and entirely proper. My question as to who has the right to be present when someone dies has now also been answered, at last. Whoever can give warmth and affection to the dying in the face of death belongs there. This is how these matters should be measured.

Troxler tells the police in a business-like tone that this is an unusual death and that the family would be grateful if the officers did not drive up in their official car but in an unmarked vehicle. They have plenty of practice and they do it well. Troxler's concern focuses on the prosecutor. Depending on who is on duty, the formalities are dealt with quickly or there will be a protracted process. The deciding factor will be how the official feels about assisted dying.

I then call Bettina and tell her that Father died with dignity and free of pain. Afterwards, I contact Angela, too. She, like all who had known that my father wanted to die this morning, must have felt that the time before they received my phone call was endlessly long. Waiting, presuming, not knowing what exactly is happening is harder to bear than being present. Martin calls his family in Nepal. And then there is also Mathias and Fabian, Evelyne, Tobias Stolte – those in on the secret. They had been waiting for nothing other than this call all morning and had perhaps secretly hoped that Father would, after all, come to a different decision. My father would no doubt have called this the 'Implementation notification'.

Again, I become aware of how difficult it will be to keep Father's death secret. This neighbourhood has eyes: people who take their dogs around the block register every irregularity, whatever the cause, as if they had nothing else to do, and then there are the postmen, gardeners, tradesmen and builders. Once a message has been fed into the net of private and business relationships, it circulates rapidly. How can we satisfy Father's most recent wish for a funeral among family and close friends only? I am annoyed about Martin's calm – in my view he does not want to see the crumbling dams. And I get even more angry with myself: why can I not let matters take their own course? Instead of letting the day have its grandeur, I spoil it with hassle and minor matters.

It must have been shortly before noon when two policemen ring the doorbell. They have arrived in an unmarked car. The older one, around forty, introduces himself and his colleague briefly expresses his condolences and asks to see the body. I lead him to the group of chairs. Police Constable Scheurer has a quick look, greets Martin and Ralph Troxler, issues a couple of instructions to his younger colleague and turns to me again:

'Was your father seriously ill? What was wrong with him?'

These questions come as a big surprise. Surely everything is clear. What else is there to ask? I feel accused, as if I had to be on my guard so that I do not say the wrong thing. It is less the words used than the direct approach the officer takes to ask his questions. My father would have called it 'frontal assault'. I am speechless for two or three seconds.

Troxler steps in.

'I have prepared all the documents. They are over there on the dining room table.'

'That is good, but I would still like to have an answer to my question from him.'

This sounds hostile in my ears:

118

'Father had a bad fall a few weeks ago for the second time and has struggled to get back to normal. The catheter for his bladder has also caused him considerable pain.'

What else should I have said to the policeman? 'Father had had enough of life. It did not run the way he wanted it to anymore. No, he did not suffer from incurable cancer; no, there was no threat of dementia coming on. Father was simply fed up with life. Do you understand this?'

Scheurer is, for the time being, satisfied with the information provided. He instructs his colleague to take pictures of the location, and he turns towards Troxler and the completed forms. The two officers take up a lot of space, more than they should, in my view. It does not help that I am telling myself that they are only doing their job. The doorbell rings again and this time it is the medical officer. After the respectful silence, there is now a frenzy of activity, which is hard to bear. Doctor Widmer informs us that he has to examine the body and that our presence is not welcome. Scheurer adds that this investigation is often very stressful for the family and he urges us to leave the apartment during this time, or at least to stay in the kitchen. If we did not object, they would like to examine the body on the carpet in front of the sofa, and he asks whether we perhaps had a large blanket or a plastic sheet.

Back in the kitchen, Troxler explains to us that the doctor and the police have a duty to examine the body all over for signs of possible use of force. They are specifically looking for places where needles might have been used to give injections. It could, theoretically, be the case that the dead person had been made compliant through the administering of a drug beforehand. He said he had heard that in criminal cases puncture sites could often be found between the toes. I do not want to hear this, and the notion that Father's body was lying naked on the floor, exposed to the officers' professional glances, makes me furious. These people, I think, are not part of this; they do not have the right to be present on the day of my father's death. Then I tell myself again and again that my father is dead and that this does not matter anymore. While Katharina Derungs, Ralph Troxler, Martin and I are waiting in the kitchen, the doorbell rings. I leave the kitchen to open the door. Out of the corner of my eye, I see Father's pale legs on a transparent plastic cover. The rest of the body remains hidden from me, behind the living room wall. I prefer it this way. The public prosecutor, Zehnder, is at the door. In contrast to the police officers, he gives the impression of being in control and able to deal with the situation. While he goes to Dr Widmer, I return to the kitchen, eyes firmly fixed on the ground in front of me. Troxler appears relieved that Zehnder is on duty – he has worked with him before and finds him quite sensible.

Five minutes later, Scheurer enters the kitchen with the glass containing the remnants of the fatal potion and hands it over to me.

'You'd better rinse this; we do not need it anymore.'

He wants to know from me where the bruise on Father's head comes from.

'He fell over four weeks ago.'

'I see.'

'The hospital can easily confirm this.'

'That's fine. These things are difficult to assess in older people.'

'Father was taking blood-thinning medication.'

'How would you like us to dress your father now?'

'Excuse me?'

'How would you like us to dress your father, now that we have finished?'

'I would like you to dress him as he was before.'

'Including the tie?'

'No, you can leave the tie.'

A few moments later, we are allowed to leave the kitchen. They have laid Father back on the sofa. His jacket is buttoned up carelessly; the clothes that Frau Derungs had arranged so lovingly are now twisted, full of creases and crumpled. He did not deserve this; she did not deserve this. I want these people to leave at long last and for calm to return.

*

After that, there is a gap in my memory. I do remember that Public Prosecutor Zehnder told me that he had once heard a talk by my father and how impressed he had been: he had found him an extraordinarily brilliant speaker. Yes, for him there was no doubt about Father's assisted dying: the situation was clear and the story consistent. I also recall staring at the cardboard fact sheet headed 'Important names and telephone numbers', which the police officers hand to me as they leave the flat. The words 'you were looked after by' are printed on it and a business card with Officer

Scheurer's name and contact details is stuck into one of the notches on the instruction pamphlet. Someone has called the undertaker, too. I believe it was Scheurer, because I remember a conversation between him and my brother. Martin tried to explain the situation to him, particularly our wish for discretion. He asked for an inconspicuous vehicle, which could perhaps come through the underground garage and points out that the transport of the body in the coffin through the staircase could be noticed. 'What do you want?' Scheurer retorts. 'Do you want them to carry your father downstairs wrapped in an old rug?'

It is lunch time now and the men from the funeral parlour will not come before early afternoon. What has Frau Derungs been doing all this time and has Troxler left? My stomach rumbles.

The next thing I remember is checking that the hearse will fit into the garage. Near the door, I run into a neighbour who is returning from walking her dog. I cannot escape her and she asks how my father is. 'Not very well', I answer. She hopes that it is nothing serious and adds that she had seen Dr Widmer park in front of the house. I tell her that it was a case of 'wait and see', but that my father would not want to receive visitors right now, in any case. Is it just my impression, or do I sound unconvincing? What more could anyone demand of me, though? I am shaken, hungry and already focusing again on keeping everything under control. How on earth do we keep Father's death a secret until after the funeral?

Thirty minutes later, the undertakers arrive. They have come in through the underground garage, unobtrusively – if a long grey estate car without windows in the back can be classified as 'unobtrusive'. And provided that the neighbours have not witnessed, through their spyholes, how the coffin was carried down the stairs. The older chap expresses his condolences warmly and tells me that he had known my father. They had occasionally met on a walk. He explains that he is still riding horses and knew that Father was an old enthusiast ever since he had done his military service in the cavalry. Oh yes, my father had been a very good man. He wondered whether it was okay with us if they took him away now or if we needed a bit more time. None of us need more time. At least we do not need more time with Father's lifeless body. Seeing the hearse leave gives me a sense of relief, not because I could not bear Father's body anymore, but because I do not have to worry that a neighbour will suddenly turn up in the apartment.

Once again, there is silence throughout the flat. But who is there to share it with? Who else except Martin is still here? Have Ralph Troxler and Katharina Derungs really left already? How did we say goodbye to each other? I do not know. I can remember the telephone ringing and one of my father's former colleagues, who had been a friend for a very long time, asking after him. He was not well, I responded, and he was not able to receive calls right now. And then I blurt out something that should never have been said: 'Can I pass on a message?' These lies, again! To be honest, the time for silent memories is now over. If I lie through my teeth, I cheat the people who are concerned about my father and whom I really like. My fib in the garage was the moment when I was caught out and could no longer pretend.

I remember going to the local parish. The clerk who was on duty in the registry office asked Martin and me to be patient for a bit: there had been 'so much dying' today, indeed all week, that they were at their limit. While I sit and wait, I browse through official pamphlets with information on births, marriages, relocation, registration for foreigners… as well as a flyer about recycling, which has somehow found its way into the registry office. My thoughts are erratic: I am thinking of Father's final words, then, seconds later, of the question which floral decoration best suited my father, only to return to childhood memories straightaway. After a quarter of an hour, Peter Borchert has time for us. He appears easy going and talkative, but provides us with the information we need and assures us of the greatest possible confidentiality, when he learns how my father died. And he delights in telling us that, in his day, Ralph Troxler had been the pastor at his confirmation. In my grief, I find Borchert too jolly and insensitive, but have to admit to myself that, at the same time, his 'business-as-usual' mentality is good for me.

*

Ordering the funeral meal in the restaurant, booking the church, organising the flowers (no wreaths!) and the music, informing the health insurance and pension provider – a never-ending list of tasks to be done by Martin, Angela and myself over the following days. These the same necessities and actions for all surviving dependants – but with the added burden of having to keep everything secret.

The secretiveness worries me. There cannot be any question of grieving yet. Persevering, being careful that no holes are torn into the net of silence and reticence, meticulously checking every detail of the necessary formalities for suspicious trails. Six days full of grim doggedness from which Angela and Martin cannot liberate me. Can we send out the texts for the death announcement to the newspapers yet? What if the publishing company passes on the information to the in-house editorial team? I have heard that this is normal because whoever has the news first is one step ahead of the others, and many papers clearly profit from this. Have we given the owner of the Restaurant Sternen too many clues when we booked the table?

On the fifth day after Father's death, one day before the ceremony in church, the net tears, despite all efforts. In line with my advice, Tobias Stolte informs a lawyer that my father has died in order to stop some business transaction that was pending. I assume that a lawyer is subject to attorney–client privilege and we can therefore take this risk. I am under a misapprehension. The lawyer informs his colleague in chambers, who has good relations with my father's previous employer. The management immediately decides to publish a death announcement in the paper the very next day. Instead of being able to grieve, I am boiling with rage. In my fury, I am determined to bring an action against this self-righteous solicitor who, without consultation, perhaps even meaning well, exceeded his authority. I have no proof, however. Father's previous employer is not prepared to release the source of the indiscretion. At least he delays the publication of the death announcement by a day.

Even now, I do not know why I kept stubbornly insisting on a small funeral. Father did, after all, leave it up to us. During the final months of his life, he decided several times both in favour and against: when he was sick of the chattering around him, he longed for a modest celebration with close friends and family. When he found himself in the centre and in public view, a grander affair seemed more appropriate. People who need rituals to say goodbye should not be deprived of such ceremonies. I am sure people would have come in droves.

Mother had wanted a funeral with only a few people present – good friends of hers – but we had been too careless over communication. Within hours, many acquaintances learnt that she had died and at that point we tried to limit the numbers. When pressed, however, we gave out details of place and time. As a result, there were two separate groups in church. There was bad blood, because some of her friends sat in the first row and others, who had not been invited, had to sit further back. This may be why I now react disproportionately to losing control and why I try to prevent indiscretions at all costs.

One of the reasons for Father's final decision to have a small celebration among close friends was his belief that guests who were not in the know might ask embarrassing questions at the funeral. He feared that the Reverend Ralph Troxler might be recognised and unmasked as a member of the assisted dying organisation. And because Father was not able to assess the reaction to him taking his own life, he worried to the end that this act could be interpreted as cowardice, a notion that he found unbearable.

Your fear is unfounded: nobody has said anything disparaging. You have irritated a few individuals, but most people are full of respect. Many think you are courageous, and those who know you feel that your death was in keeping with your life. You see, your image has remained unscathed.

This secretiveness has robbed the days following Father's death of much dignity. I, too, believe many need a particular place, a firm ritual and the close contact with like-minded people in their grieving. Martin and I had decided, for our moments of remembrance, not to share our father with the kind of public we shared him with during our lifetime.

*

On the day of the funeral, spring shows its cool and rainy side. At seven o'clock in the morning, we leaf through the newspaper. It had worked: the announcement of Father's death has not been published. Only those 'on the inside' will be at the ceremony, i.e. only those who had known before how Father would die.

The eight o'clock news bulletin reports his death and there is a short appreciation of his life. A tabloid is mentioned as the source. Martin buys a copy at a kiosk and we find an obituary, with picture, in the editorial section. There is no word about the day of his death. Two acquaintances call my mobile, as does the office of the Rotary Club: they would like to know the time of the funeral and where they can send a wreath.

I sit in the car outside the church, heavy raindrops falling on the window and running down the pane. I switch my phone to silent and try to compose myself. Two days ago, the big fir tree at the church entrance had been cut down – it had provided shelter from the rain when I had been confirmed. People walking past had been shocked; a part of what had been so familiar to them had been taken away. I get out and am relieved: 'It is too late', I think, 'you can write and say what you want to. The ceremony will start in thirty minutes. We'll be just us.'

In the two front rows there are twelve people who were close to my father in the last few days of his life. The church bells ring out and then one after the other falls silent. For the first time since Father's death, I feel a deep inner peace. No threatening phone calls, no tactical manoeuvring and weighing up pros and cons, no lies. At this moment, there is only him and me – and my emotion – which brings tears to my eyes. One of Father's favourite songs, 'Ave Maria', is played on the flute, and afterwards the Reverend Ralph Troxler recounts his life. He finds the right words, because he was close to Father in life and in death. I am grateful. The organist plays Schubert's 'Impromptu' on the grand piano. It is really Mother's song, but my father listened to it time and again after her death. It is appropriate for this celebration. An uninvited photographer scurries past in the back of the church. He must have discovered where the funeral would take place, but has to accept that he has come in vain: there are no celebrities whose pictures could fill the pages of the tabloids the next day.

I have decided to say a few words, too. I thought Father would like it if a member of the family said goodbye. It is a chance for me to give him a voice once more: in the weeks before his death, Father wrote three poems, which deal with the journey from this world to the next. I read one of them.

Father always had a clear notion of the end of his funeral. In his army days, the trumpeter played 'Il Silenzio' to the unit at the end of the day, while the flag was lowered. Afterwards, there must be silence. This was what he wished for his funeral service, too. The trumpeter takes up his position quietly and unobtrusively next to Father's urn and coaxes sounds of almost boundless purity from his instrument.

It is quiet, and you are in our midst.

Two other books set in Switzerland, also translated by Iris Hunter and published by Perfect Publishers:

Marcella Maier
The Green Silk Shawl

Marcella Maier weaves the fascinating stories of her female ancestors on and around a green silk shawl that is handed down from mother to daughter.

This book is for everyone with an interest in the development of modern Europe and with the possibilities of oral history. Through the memories of successive generations of Swiss women, we relive Napoleon's marauding troops, early industrial action by washer women wanting better wages, the introduction of electricity (this 'work of the devil'), the beginnings of tourism and of a health service, as well as the deprivation brought by two world wars. The author's understated style brilliantly conveys the women's stoicism and their calm fortitude in the face of adversity: they sought solutions without complaint and just got on with their incredibly tough, but somehow affirming, lives.

https://www.thegreensilkshawl.co.uk/
This book is also available in electronic format.

Ulrich Knellwolf
Death in Sils Maria

This is another book set in the Engadin.

The idyllic village in the Swiss mountains with its iconic luxury hotel is not what it seems: some of the guests do not have relaxation and winter sport on the minds – but murder.

Death comes in many guises and in the most unlikely locations: in the cosy surroundings of hotel bars, on sunlit ski slopes and on thin ice.

At last, connoisseurs of crime fiction all over the world can enjoy an English translation of these evocative tales of dark foreboding. This book makes a wonderful travel companion, and those who stay at home by the fire will enter a fascinating world of passion and revenge.

Ulrich Knellwolf, a true master of irony and the tongue-in-cheek, has produced a captivating collection of wicked page-turners.

www.deathinsilsmaria.co.uk
This book is also available in electronic format and as an audiobook.